Introduc

My name is Peter Gentles, at the time of w
have been retired for some three years. I we .... up in the
South Side of Glasgow, at a time when there were hardly any cars, and my
dad used to send me across Allison Street, to Stewart Campbells off licence
to buy him cigarettes, 20 Kensitas plain at two shillings and eleven pence
ha'penny! I was aged about four or five!

I recently drove along Allison Street, wouldn't want to live there now I'm
afraid...

What ensues in this book are anecdotes, memories, events and tons of
other stuff that occurred in my forty-eight years in the trade.

I will endeavour to not use big words when a singularly loquacious and
diminutive expression will satisfactorily accomplish the contemporary
necessity.

I have changed the names of some of the people, mainly because what
I recount about them may not be favourable, or indeed true, and living
on my pension, I cannot afford to be sued, or indeed engage in any legal
battles whatsoever!

I must also say that what I have written is how I remember things, and
may or may not have happened quite as described, although I'm pretty
sure what follows is as near as dammit to what actually happened, if that
makes sense...

Anyway, I hope you enjoy my ramblings as much as I have enjoyed writing
them...

Contents

Chapter One - In the Beginning...

My dad used to run Johnstones Garage in Garturk Street, Govanhill. which at the time was a Rootes dealership, but they had several Rolls-Royces, which in the early sixties, you could hire to take you into town, at a cost of half a crown, or twelve and a half pence in todays money. I was born in 272 Allison Street, which was round the corner from the garage in the south side of Glasgow.

Myself and Lenny Thomson at Johnstones Garage in
Garturk Street. Lenny tragically took his own life,
as his wife Meg was terminally ill. The two of them
were separated only by death.................

I grew up in that garage, spending my time in there after school, in fact, I learned to ride my first bicycle (which was second hand and far too big for me) by standing on the running boards of a RR, (It may have been a 20/25), launching myself off, and cycling round the block, to come back to the same car to enable me to alight!

This may have been where my love of motor cars came about.

I always remember the two mechanics, Jock Berry and Jock Murray, typical of the times, both smoked pipes, and their boiler suits could stand up by themselves!

I also remember running around the workshop, pushing a trolley full of gear oil….never a good idea! The trolley overturned (I took a bend too fast) and spilled the oil all over the workshop floor…dad wasn't pleased to say the least!

The garage was massive, in those days people and tradesmen could park their cars inside overnight, and had a key for access…..changed days of trust now.

One such "lodger" was the Welcome fireplace lorry, which according to my dad, he always made sure there was sand in the back for me to play in. The lorry also served as a useful launching pad for the rope swing I made, tied to the roof trusses of the garage. No fear in those days!

Move forward to around 1967, we lived in Cordiner Street in Mount Florida, and a local businessman (Leslie Blass, a clothing manufacturer, long gone and his premises is now a pub called Clockwork) used to park his Bentley outside my mum and dads house, and I have a photograph of me, age about 12, standing next to it. I believe it was either an S1 or S2. My goals were set – I wanted to be involved with cars, and a mechanic was now my dream job.

I had to content myself in the meantime. My friend Robin's mother was secretary to Reo Stakis at the time, and managed to procure us both a job on Saturdays, manning the door of the Casino Chevalier. We sat behind the desk at the front, and would unlock the door if anyone that looked official appeared. This rarely happened, I think it was just to give us something to do, but we had a great time…mostly spent in the casino playing with the roulette tables, and in the kitchen making chips followed by ice cream! I vaguely remember one of Reo Stakis's sons getting chased by some boys, all around our ages, and we let his son in and chased the ruffians away!

I had two part-time jobs at the age of fourteen. I worked for the co-operative in Cathcart Road, Mount Florida, delivering groceries every afternoon, after school, Monday to Friday. Every Saturday morning I worked in the shop, serving in the fruit and veg section. That's where I learned to juggle, usually potatoes, but sometimes oranges, just as long as they weren't damaged when I dropped them! Apples were a no-no! The wages weren't great, but the tips were good, one regular, Mrs Munn in particular used to give me half a crown (Twelve and a half pence nowadays). Not bad, when I was getting eight shillings (forty pence) a week, only trouble was she lived four stories up, and always had a heavy egg box crammed with groceries! (Egg box not to be confused with X box, which is something totally different!) On Saturdays I was paid extra.

I also worked in the speedway when it was a Hampden Park stadium (1969 to 1972), on a Friday night. The task was to "squeegee" the grit back to the inside of the track after every race, anyone who has ever watched speedway will know exactly what I mean.

If you were a regular, there was a chance you were "promoted" to pushing the speedway bikes to get them started. Pay was eight shillings (40p) for the evening. I loved that job, I could watch the racing for nothing, and get paid!
In 1969, I also rode for the Hampden Hawks, a cycle speedway team. I was into photography at that time, and took many pictures of the riders racing on the Saturday, and flog them the following Saturday. Many of my photos are still doing the rounds.

The Hampden hawks in 1969
Myself in bottom left

Left to Right:

Myself, Nicky and David Norrie
at one of our reunions.

To be noted that we are all about
3 stone above our racing weight!

I also took all the passport photographs for the school trip, developing them at night and taking them in the next day. That was lucrative, a right few bob was earned!

My dad was transport manager at Security Express in Kinning Park, based in a huge railway yard. I used to go in with my dad every Saturday morning, and he would give me the keys to one of the Bedford HA (Viva) vans, and this was how I learned to drive at an early age.
I also brought in food for a stray cat which lived there, and he used to wait every Saturday morning and run to me. When my dad was made redundant, I had to take the cat with us, and I named him Fred, just to wind up our next door neighbour who was also named Fred!

Many years later, I had my own Silver Cloud 1, and have a photograph of me standing beside it, and also one next to my mum and dads house, just like back in 1967.

Me beside the Bentley at 29 Cordiner Street

Left and Right Me with my Silver Cloud

I wanted to leave school at 15 years old, which you could do in those days. I was talked (pressurised more like) into staying on to sit my "O" levels, I was considered quite clever, so why I wanted to be a mechanic I'll never know!

Our neighbour and friend across the road was quite high up in the SMTA (Scottish Motor Trade Association) and managed through his contacts to arrange an interview with A & D Fraser in Springkell Avenue, Maxwell Park. I attended the interview, and obviously my keenness must have shone through, as I was offered an apprenticeship, in the Rolls-Royce workshop! WOW!

Statement of Terms and Conditions of Employment
with
A. & D. FRASER LTD., 65 Springkell Avenue, Glasgow, S.I.

Dated ....

Employee: (Name) .... PETER GENTLES ....

.... (Address) .... 29 CORDINER STREET, CATHCART, GLASGOW, S. 4. ....

Category of Employment: .... APPRENTICE MOTOR MECHANIC ....

Date of Commencement of Employment: .... 26/7/71 .... Date of Birth .... 17/8/55 ....

Basic Wage or Salary .... £0.16250 .... per .... HOUR .... payable .... WEEKLY ....

Notice of Termination: The following periods of notice of termination of employment will apply :—

(1) When notice is given by the employer -

     a) Where the employee has been continuously employed for 26 weeks and less than two years — one week's notice.

     b) Where the employee has been continuously employed for two years and less than five years — two weeks' notice.

     c) Where the employee has been continuously employed for five years or more — four weeks' notice.

(2) When notice is given by the employee who has been continuously employed for 26 weeks or more — one week's notice.

These provisions do not prevent either party from waiving his right to notice on any occasion or from accepting a payment in lieu of notice. Nor do they effect the right of either party to treat the contract as terminable, without notice or payment in lieu of notice, by reason of such conduct by the other party as would have enabled him to do so before the passing of the Contracts of Employment Act, 1963

REMARKS:

     I acknowledge to have received a Statement of which the above is a copy together with a second sheet appropriate to my Category of Employment.

Date .... Signature ....

My terms and conditions

A & D Fraser Limited
65 Springkell Avenue
Glasgow S1
Telephone: 041-423 3011 (Parts 041-423 8841)
Telex: 77117

Directors

K D Fraser	H F Cameron
D I Fraser	W B Gilmour
E Miller	D R Moore

Our Ref: JMcL/GF

15th June, 1971

Mrs. M. Gentles,
29 Cordiner Street,
Cathcart,
Glasgow, S.4

Dear Madam,

     We acknowledge receipt of your letter dated 10th June, 1971, and would advise you that it will be in order for Peter to start with us on Monday, 23rd August, 1971.

          Yours faithfully,
       for A & D FRASER LIMITED

                    (J. McLaughlin)
                    WORKS MANAGER

Distributor for: **Morris** Retail Dealers for **MG, Wolseley, BMC Commercial**
For terms of business see over

My letter of job offer – note it is addressed to my mum…

A & D Fraser Limited
65 Springkell Avenue
Glasgow S1
Telephone : 041-423 3011 (Parts 041-423 8841)
Telex: 77117

Directors

K D Fraser	H F Cameron
D I Fraser	W B Gilmour
E Miller	D R Moore

Our Ref: JMcL/MA

18th June, 1971.

Mrs M. Gentles,
29 Cordiner Street,
CATHCART,
Glasgow, S.4

Dear Madam,

Further to our letter dated the 15/6/71 we would advise you that Peter could start with our company at any time. We wish to familiarise him with the work shop before any college enrolment would take place and we would therefore ask you if it is suitable to advise us on the earliest starting date that Peter could make. Awaiting your reply at your earliest convenience.

Yours faithfully,
for A & D FRASER LIMITED

(J.McLaughlin)
WORKS MANAGER

Distributor for: **Morris** Retail Dealers for **MG, Wolseley, BMC Commercial**
For terms of business see over

My Career had begun……………………………..

12

Chapter Two - *My first day as an apprentice...*

August 1971, I'd left Kings Park school before the Summer break, and today was my first day as an apprentice Rolls-Royce mechanic with A & D Fraser.

Shining like a new pin, I entered the world of the grown ups.....

I was introduced to my boss, a chap called John Findlay (Big John), who was to have a major influence on my skill as a mechanic. He was very hard, but also very fair – you knew exactly where you stood. Ironically, as I found out years later, his nickname when he was an apprentice was "speed", as he didn't do anything very quickly!

A & D Frasers
65 Springkell
Avenue
Maxwell Park
Glasgow
Now a housing
estate

Photograph courtesy
of
Fraser Anderson

A & D Frasers itself was a massive outfit, as you came in the main front door, there were offices to the left, fuel pumps on the right, and in that same section was car hire, and the directors offices both on the ground floor and upstairs – we were never allowed to venture there!

Next section was the RR & B workshop. It was a large workshop, with only one 4 – post ramp. That was for final inspections only, heaven help you if you used it for anything else. The workshop from memory had about 12 to 14 bays, and when I started, there were eight mechanics including 4th year apprentices. We also had our own machine shop, including a lathe, which was used among other things, to resurface brake drums on Silver Clouds and the like.

Through a door and down some steps (more on them later) was the electrical workshop, the foreman being Alan Aitken, along with Owen Duncan and John Rankin. Onto the next section, which was the British Leyland Service reception, the Sun tuning bay, run by a real character called Joe Margiotta (Hopefully that's the correct spelling) and the car washing area. Next area was the BLMC workshop, incorporating a very early form of flow line, where one mechanic worked on the top, and one under the ramps, where the servicing was carried out. Any other repairs were carried out on the surrounding floor.

Next section was the heavy repair, and by that I mean commercial vans and light trucks. Moving on, came the body shop, where accident damaged vehicles were stripped and repaired, ready for painting, the paint shop being the final area in what I reckoned to be a building quarter of a mile long.
The parts department and showroom were in a separate building, fronted by Springkell Avenue.
The whole area covered was massive, including our own football pitch and a large piece of waste ground.

Once I had been introduced to everyone, and issued with overalls, I was assigned to Martin White (or "Thatch" as he was nicknamed due to his haircut). He was servicing a Morris Marina, and asked me to flick the ignition so he could set the points. I understood "flick" differently to what Martin thought, and proceeded to spin the engine over. As Martin wasn't ready for that, his screwdriver got caught in the fan and went through the radiator! Not a great start, but he should have been more specific!
You may think it odd that there was a Morris Marina in the RR workshop, but there were several reasons why we would be working on non franchise vehicles. If we were quiet, we would take some of the load off the BLMC section, or it may be a RR/B owners second car, wifes car, or one of the directors cars, etc, as people liked the fact that a RR/B mechanic was working on their car, perceivably to a higher standard.
It was good to diversify, and gave me a broader experience. My very first solo job was to fit a set of brake shoes to one of the directors wives Mini…...work was double checked by a mechanic every step of the way, but the sense of satisfaction I felt was what it was all about!

Part of my duties though, were what every apprentice has to go through…. making tea and going to the shop. There was a shop on site which sold the usual stuff, rolls and sausage, sweets, crisps etc., but quite often, one of the mechanics would drive the tea boy to "Sweaty Bettys", a shop minutes away which did the best rolls and sausage with tattie scone.

I had to take the orders make the tea, go to the shop and come back with everything correct. Woe betide me if I got it wrong, I would have to go back to the shop, and get the correct stuff, sometimes forfeiting my own tea break. Soon learned to get it right, and also to make a "skin" from the money.

Tea breaks were spent sitting on toolboxes or anything you could find to park your bum on, including the running boards of a V12 Phantom 111, which apparently had been there for years waiting on a camshaft – no luxury of a proper canteen! When the Phantom eventually was moved, the tyres had stuck to the floor and had to be towed out with our Land Rover, due to the fact over the years, everyone had been throwing the dregs of their tea underneath it!

Friday afternoons after lunch, the apprentices scrubbed the concrete floor with caustic soda! Wouldn't be tolerated today due to health and safety regulations, something unheard of then!

The mechanics would spend the afternoon delivering cars, and one other lad would go round and collect them, usually in the bosses Morris Marina. No luxury of dedicated drivers then! Again in todays motor trade, this would not be tolerated as if affects the "technicians" (as they are now called) productive efficiency.

A good technician or master technician commands a very healthy salary, so drivers on just above living wage are a more cost effective option. Good drivers are worth their weight in gold, as it is often forgotten that they are the only point of contact with some customers, and can make or break a relationship. I have been very fortunate with my drivers, great guys, and often undervalued, but more of that later.

As there were no ramps we could use, the apprentices job was to jack the car up, with the rather large workshop jacks. The car would be about 3 feet in the air, then supported by big axle stands.

The apprentice would remove the wheels and brake drums if it was pre Shadow, drain the engine oil and change the oil filter – none of those screw off/on filters, they had to be stripped and cleaned out in a paraffin bath, and a replacement paper element and seals fitted. The brakes were "blown out" with compressed air which resulted in the workshop being engulfed in a cloud of asbestos dust, which if it became too bad, we would stand outside until it cleared a wee bit! Health and Safety? It's a wonder I'm still alive (touching wood as I write).

From memory, there were some 27 grease points on a Cloud or S Type, and apart from the three on the prop shaft, the rest were pumped full of "Rocol" grease, which was the stickiest, mankiest, and most horrible stuff to work with. We didn't have the luxury of disposable gloves then.

The mechanics sole duties on a service were to clean or replace the plugs and points, and clean out the carburettors. The carburettors were often cleaned in an open bath of petrol, made out of a cut in half gallon tin can. They were then polished with Brasso or T cut. He would then check and adjust the ignition timing using a test lamp, while the apprentice lay on the floor, turning the flywheel with a screwdriver until the timing marks lined up.

If one of the more senior mechanics, ie the chargehand were to road test a car, the overalls would get taken off, the comb would come out and the hair would be neatly combed. The Rolls-Royce or Bentley would then be road tested, with the mechanic making out that maybe he owned the car to anyone who noticed. This was known as "Kinging it", some may say lording it or just posing!
Not all members of the public appreciated these cars, sometimes they would spit at the car, or shout abuse...morons!

If you were lucky, (or unlucky depending on your point of view!) Big John would take you out on road test with him....route would usually be along the Kennishead Road, a twisty, windy A class road where speed limits were unheard of (or perhaps just ignored!).
From memory, Big John was some driver, he could make a Silver Cloud do things you wouldn't believe was possible.

I remember once overhauling the braking system on a Silver Shadow, and John took me out for the road test. This time, we went on the motorway past Glasgow airport, doing well over 100mph, when someone slammed on the brakes in front of us….Big John did the same and the Shadow screeched to a halt….cool as a cucumber Big John said "at least you got the brakes working – good job! No such thing as ABS in the mid seventies.

Thanks to Fraser Anderson, (sales manager at the time with A & D Fraser) for the photograph of the old place.
I had the pleasure to recently meet up with Fraser, and we had a good catch up about old times, and he gave me a good few photographs, some of which will be featured in subsequent chapters.

As part of my apprenticeship, I would be attending college, firstly on day release to Langside College, then subsequently block release to LAGTA (Lanarkshire Automobile Group Training Association) in Coatbridge. My nickname was "Rollsy" (amongst other names!), due to the fact I was working in the Rolls-Royce shop. I would also attend Springburn college of Engineering. That resulted in my first driving ban, as I had a car at the time, a 1963 Ford Anglia 105E, but only a provisional licence. I would say to my mum that I was away for the bus, but would go to my lock-up and get the car. All was well, until one day, driving home from Springburn, I was sitting at traffic lights, and must have looked guilty as two police officers passed by.

Given an order to produce my licence resulted in me getting caught. I was charged with no "L" plates and no accompanying qualified driver. I was banned for 3 months two weeks after passing my driving test……

This was to be an insight into my horrendous driving convictions in the coming few years...
The custom on Hogmanay (New Years Eve) was that big John brought in a carry oot, and we all finished early and retired to the machine shop, where we had a wee party. Not being able to drive enabled me to partake of a little drinky-poo, and I had to be carried home by Thatch, who dropped me off at my house and buggered off before my mum came out!

I was also attending MOTEC, (Multi-Occupational Training and Educational Centre, later renamed CENTREX) college in Livingston, which had a bar and snooker hall, mainly for the delegates who had live in accommodation.

They opened the bar at lunchtimes, never a good move. Myself and another lad missed an exam as we were playing snooker and lost track of time. That didn't go down well with my employer, but arrangements were made to resit the exam, glad to say I passed it!

Welcome to the world of Rolls-Royce And Bentley…...

Chapter Three - A & D Frasers bought over by Appleyard...

Shortly after I joined A & D's they were bought over by the Appleyard group. Didn't affect us much, just a change of name.
Head office was now in Leeds, which takes me on to my next recollection a couple of years down the line...

I had just dropped my mum and dad at the bus station, as they were away on holiday, then went to work.
One of the directors was late for a meeting in Leeds, and had left some important papers behind, essential to this meeting. My boss, John Findlay, knew I was an "enthusiastic" driver, and gave me the keys to a Triumph TR7, fairly fast sports car (in its day!). "Peter", he said, "take these documents to Head office, as quickly as you can".

It was in the days before the M74, so cruising down the A74, at approx 110mph, I overtook a coach full of holidaymakers, a wee bit later, I had to slow down a wee bit for the long sweeping right hander just as you come into Dumfries and Galloway, too late to spot the police traffic car sitting in the lay-by, pointing their radar detector at me! I was duly pulled in, and was standing talking to the police while they gave me a speeding ticket, fortunately sub 100mph, 98mph to be exact.

Just then the coach I had previously passed at some 110mph, passed us by, with the occupants staring and some laughing (at me presumably). I thought no more about it, delivered the papers to the receptionist in Leeds head office, then made my way back home, of course observing the speed limit (well in Dumfries and Galloway at any rate!)

It didn't quite end there, firstly, the receptionist at head office didn't pass on the papers, and secondly, around a week later, I was asking how mum and dad got on, and they told me about this reckless youngster in a sports car zoom past them, then (laughing) the police caught him – hope they threw the book at him! Guess who that reckless youngster in a sports car was?

I once had to drive a Rolls-Royce Phantom 11 I believe it was, up to Lucas auto electricians in Garscube Road. The car had an opening windscreen, and I remember passing a building being sandblasted, and somehow some sandblasting grit found its way through the windscreen into my eyes! I was blinded and managed to pull in. I was near a library, and they phoned the garage, who sent out a couple of guys to take me to accident and emergency, and to take the car to Lucas. That car, I believe is now in the Glasgow museum of transport.

We were to move our operation a couple of times with Appleyard, first to Crow Road, just at the Southern exit to the Clyde Tunnel, then onto the old Callanders Mercedes site at Kirklee Road, in the West End.

In Kirklee Road we were also Jaguar, and big John asked me if I fancied working on a fire engine. Sure, that's a bit different, no problem. Some of these fire engines exhibited overheating issues, and as they had 4.2 Jaguar engines, it was left to us to investigate the problem.

It was a bit of a nightmare, as the engine was located centrally under the crew seating area, which made it awkward. First I had to remove the cylinder head, only to find a crack between number 3 and number 4 cylinders, which meant getting a new engine. I learned a good many new swear words on that job, and eventually the replacement engine was fitted and started up.

Before handing back to the fire service, the original cause of the overheating had to be rectified, ensuring it wouldn't happen again.
This involved fitting a series of cooling ducts, thus directing cool air to the inboard radiator. I had to test the vehicle which I did, but was not allowed to use the "blues and twos", which I'm afraid I did, as my hand slipped onto the switch!

We never did any more fire engines, thankfully, as we were just the guinea pigs to find out what needed to be done.

Some of the perks….

I remember that Slade were in town, playing at the Apollo. They had an issue with the exhaust manifold gaskets blowing on their Rolls-Royce Phantom VI, and I was given the job of sorting it while the roadie waited! The place was buzzing, and word spread like wildfire that we had Slade's car in. Downside was that the exhaust was roasting, but with my asbestos hands, I managed to replace the gaskets.

When I was finishing off, the roadie came up to me and after thanking me, said "would I like tickets for tonight's gig?", to which I replied "Who's playing?" Didn't go down to well, but I got the tickets anyway. That was probably the first concert I'd ever been to, went with my girlfriend, later to become my wife. What a concert, I loved Slade in any case, but to see and hear them live was amazing. The atmosphere in the Apollo was awesome.

Maybe around 1977, my boss, John Findlay gave me two tickets for a Demis Roussos concert that evening, as he had something else on. Again, we went to the Apollo venue. We were shown up to these rubbish seats right at the back of the venue. All we could see was this black dot in the distance. We lasted until the intermission, at which point we went to leave. The doorman commented if we left, we wouldn't be allowed back in, which suited us fine. Demis Roussos is (or was) an acquired taste.

I was the chargehand mechanic (yes, we were mechanics in those days!), and part of my trusted duties would include driving the Leyland Terrier transporter.

It was 1979, and the call came in to my boss, John Findlay, could Appleyards transport the priceless 1905 3 Cylinder Rolls-Royce (The Old Girl) from Doune Motor Museum to Duxford Airfield in Cambridge, for the Rolls-Royce on wheel and wing 75th anniversary celebrations on the 16th of September…..no hesitation on that one then! I had the privilege of being chosen to make the run, and loaded up SD 661 at the museum, under the Eagle Eye of Jim Wardaw, who had the honour of being the cars custodian. The car was stored under cover that night at Appleyard's premises, ready for an early start the next morning.

The next morning, accompanied by Jim and Mrs Wardlaw, we set off for Duxford, and had a very pleasant drive down, although certainly not breaking any speed records!

The Old Girl (the car, not Mrs W!) was unloaded and stored in one of the hangars under lock and key overnight. We then checked into our hotel and had dinner, then a drink in the bar.

It had been a long day, so after a few yawns, it was decided to call it a night, so we retired. I gave it around 20 minutes, and I went back down to the bar, to find Jim, who had the same idea!

Next day, back to the airfield for what was a fantastic day, and one I will remember for ever. So much to see, wonderful cars, wonderful aircraft, and a great bunch of people….I even had the honour of being a passenger in the Old Girl….,

The time came to conclude the event, and the car was loaded back onto the transporter, for the return home the next day. Next day proved to be somewhat inclement to say the least, but the Old Girl (the car, not Mrs W) was warm and dry under a cover (or so we thought).

Not a great trip back in torrential rain, but made it in one piece back to Appleyards. On removal of the cover, every piece of brass on the car had tarnished with the moisture!!

Lots of Brasso required for Jim once we returned to Doune the following day….great memories, of which in my 48 years with Rolls-Royce and Bentley, I have many, many more.

Next page…..

That's me in the grey dustcoat loading the "Old Girl" onto our Leyland Terrier transporter. Excuse the quality of the pics, they were converted from slides, but are also donkeys years old!
The "Old Girl" now resides in the Glasgow Riverside Museum...

I had bought an Austin Healey Sprite Mk1 (Frogeye) which was an ex racing car, so had uprated brake discs, Minilite wheels and all the race trimmings, but they had removed the race engine and substituted it with an 848cc Austin A40 unit. Wouldn't pull the skin off a rice pudding, so had to go. Appleyard at the time were a British Leyland special tuning dealer, so I was able to purchase the necessary tuning gear at a good discount, but first I needed a good 1275cc A Series unit as a base.

This was duly acquired from the warranty section, substituting it with my old 848 unit.

I had it bored out to 1298cc, and my boss allowed me to work several Saturday mornings in the workshop, polishing and porting the cylinder head I had also acquired. An almost race engine was duly built and fitted....I loved that wee car.

I got my first Jaguar when I was about 21. It was a series 1 XJ6, 4.2 litre in Regency Red. I bought it from a friends dad, and me and my pal Brian spent a full day bulling it up ("detailing" in todays speak!). AYS817K was its registration number, shortly to be replaced by VSD10, which I got from an old Austin Cambridge I had bought for £18, sold the wheels for £5, and scrapped the car.

Working on Rolls-Royces, I had "access" to an 8 track quadraphonic player, which was duly installed in the Jag. We had to fit an extra two speakers, so it was decided they would go in the rear doors. I was to do one side and Brian was to do the other side. Speakers fitted, but only issue was one was at the front of the rear door trim, and the other one was at the rear of the door trim! Distinct lack of communication I fear! It did however remain thus for the remainder of my ownership, and sounded incredible.

I was driving along Carmunnock road one day, when an elderly gentleman in a Volvo pulled out of a side street, right into my precious Jag! His fault, his insurance, car was recovered into our bodyshop at Springkell Avenue. For once, I didn't have any other cars about me, so a deal was struck with Nigel at Budget Rent a Car, which was part of our garage. At finishing time every day, I would go and see what Nigel had for me to use, it could be anything from a Mini to a van, I didn't care, as long as I was mobile. This went on for a few weeks while my car was sorted. For that privilege, I would bung Nigel a fiver ever week. Cheaper than putting petrol in the Jag!

I met my first wife when I had one of the minis, so at least I know she wasn't after me for the Jaguar!

My next Jaguar was a Series 2 Jaguar XJ12, with a knackered engine. I'd sold my previous Series 1 XJ6 to one of my mates. We had a Landrover and trailer, which I was allowed to use it to collect the Jaguar. The Landrover had its own driver, who came with me, and "secured" the car onto the trailer. I remarked at the time is it secure, to which the driver replied "of course it is, don't tell me my job!"

First set of lights at red, the Jaguar came adrift and ran over the trailer winch, damaging the front of the car and the oil cooler. Just hard lines, as they were doing me a favour….

Big John allowed me to bring the car into the workshop at weekends to do what needed done to the engine. I stripped the V12 engine, overhauled it, including re-grinding the crankshaft. All duly built up and running great, until that is, around 10,000 miles later, the big ends went. Bugger, that's all I needed.

Appleyard was at the time also a Jaguar dealer (that's handy). I mentioned my predicament to Martin Routlage, who was the Jaguar area service manager. He was surprised that the engine had lasted 10,000 miles, as once the crankshaft is reground, it destroys the case hardening…now he tells me. He picked up the phone and called his head office. Conversation went something like this:

Martin: Remember that XJS engine in Inverness? It's scrap, can Appleyard have it to train their apprentices?

Jaguar Head Office: OK

Martin then said to me, borrow a van and pick up that engine at the weekend from Inverness.

There is nothing wrong with it, they replaced the engine for a knocking noise, turns out the fault was with the air conditioning compressor! Result! The engine came out an XJS with only 1,100 miles. Only condition was that Martin would keep the fuel injection system, which suited me as my car had carburettors.

Done and dusted, engine fitted and all hunky dory. Martin would not accept anything for this, just buy him a gin and tonic next time we meet. Martin also got me a set of XJS alloy wheels, which had very slight marking and were replaced under warranty.

I fulfilled my end of the bargain, and bought him a large G&T at our works night out!

I eventually sold the car to a pal, along with the "VSD10" registration number, which I got an extra £400 for. I then used that £400 to buy 914PG from Nino Verrico, which I still have to this day, now on my Z4.

When we were in our premises in Crow Road, being British Leyland as well, there was a television advertising campaign, which was filmed in our dealership. Afraid to say it was Jimmy Saville who fronted the ad, my pal Jimmy McGuinness even shook hands with the guy! Best forgotten now I reckon.

About this time, I was introduced to the Casino, the Chevalier to be exact. This resulted in me getting a bit hooked on gambling, culminating in one Friday night, I lost quite heavily, keeping money aside for a taxi home, losing that but keeping enough for a bus home, then losing that and walking home. I had blown all my wages, so promised myself, never again and stuck to that, although later visiting the casino, but only for a meal.

I also used to frequent night clubs, and particular the Warehouse in Glasgow city centre. This resulted in me burning the candle at both ends, so much so that one day at work, I put a Silver Shadow up on the ramp, sat inside and fell asleep. I was rudely awakened by big John Findlay tearing me a new arsehole. I had learned another lesson.

I had my Suzuki 850 motorbike, and used to give one of the apprentices a lift to work. I nicknamed him "Shaking Stevens" as when I took the long sweeping right hander going onto the Kingston Bridge, he used to shake and try and lean upright which didn't help with the handling, especially as we were over a hundred feet above the river.

One time I was farting about with him on the back, and I pulled a "wheelie" and next thing I knew his legs whizzed up past my ears. I soon dropped the front back down to earth, and his legs followed suit. Neither of us had helmets on, as we were just in the works car park. Guess I was invincible in those days!

The Appleyard Team, Kirklee Road - I reckon around 1980

Back two rows left to right:
Davie Moir (parts department)
Nan Flannigan (office)
Stuart McCauley (trainee manager)
Peter Gentles (Chargehand)
Gordon Adam (Auto Electrician) nicknamed "Grizly"
Davie Burns (Mechanic)
Alfie Graham (Car cleaner) nicknamed "Wingie"
Willie Curry (Mechanic)
Ian McIntosh (Mechanic) nicknamed "Skelfie"
Bob Martin (Cost Clark) nicknamed "Piles"

Front row left to right:
Jim McGuinness (Mechanic)
Brian Collins (Apprentice Mechanic)
Dougie Crockett (Apprentice Mechanic)
John Graham (Mechanic) Dusters stuffed under his shoulders to make him look butch! Lol
Photograph courtesy of Fraser Anderson

Those of you with Silver Shadows or derivatives will be aware of how quickly the engine runs when on full choke….for those of you not familiar, it's bloody fast. Now we always made it a rule when working on these cars, that the gearchange thermal cut out was removed for safety. Shadow 1 & T1 this was located in the fuse box, next to the handbrake, and on Shadow 2/T2/Early Spirit, this was located in the fuse box at the passenger knee roll. Took seconds to remove, some people either forgetting or too lazy! Anyway, my first experience of this was in the electricians workshop in Springkell Avenue. If you recall, there was a small flight of stairs between there and our workshop. One of the electricians was working on the car with the engine running on full choke, he reached in through the drivers window, presumably to switch on the lights or something, and his sleeve caught on the column gear lever lurching the car into drive! The car hurtled forward, and climbed the steps, trying to squeeze through the door! Result was the car was a bit shorter than it used to be, in fact the chassis was bent at the front, and had to go back to the factory to get repaired, as it was too major for our bodyshop.

A similar instance happened when we were in Kirklee Road years later – same scenario, but the car was on a ramp, fortunately still at floor level. Again it was an electrician working on it, same thing happened, I saw it in slow motion, with the offending electrician trying to hold back a two and a half ton motor car. Unsuccessful in his attempt, the car carried on and demolished the big workshop heater.

Yet another incident, back to the electrical workshop and a Rover 2000. First I knew the car was on fire was John Findlay running down our workshop towards the connecting door, for a big guy, John Could move! Stopping was more difficult as he always had metal segs on the soles of his shoes, not giving a great deal of grip, but good sparks! The Rover under bonnet was ablaze, when I went through, everyone and their aunties were pointing fire extinguishers at it, but to no avail. The starter motor had shorted, causing it to keep the engine spinning over, this in turn caused the engine driven mechanical fuel pump to keep pumping out blazing petrol through the melted rubber fuel hose.

All attempts were useless, as the bonnet being open allowed plenty of oxygen to keep the fire going. I grabbed a floor brush, and whacked the bonnet stay, causing the bonnet to slam shut. This stopped the oxygen keeping the fire going, and allowed us to concentrate the extinguishers at underneath the engine. The fire was soon no more. The battery was disconnected stopping the engine. After tidying up, 29 used fire extinguishers were counted! There was no training then, unlike today.

Do you notice a recurring theme here with electricians?

I had almost completed my apprenticeship, being in my 4th year, which meant I would receive my tradesman certificate on my Birthday, 17th of August 1975, when I would reach the ripe old age of 20!
I was flattered to be given the chance to go on a training course with Rolls-Royce in London, I believe I was the first apprentice to be given that opportunity.

I was to set off on Sunday the 22nd of June 1975, as the 2 week (yes, two week!) training started the next day.
I packed my Sunbeam Stiletto with everything but the kitchen sink, and set off listening to Billy Connoly on my state of the art 8-track player. (More about Billy later)

It was a beautiful day, so I drove all the way to London with the window open, and right arm resting on the door, something I was to regret, as the next day I suffered from sunburn on my arm, or "truckers arm" as it is known! I could have got the train, but where's the fun in that at 19 years old…..

I was booked into the County Hotel in Russell Square, what a dump, shared toilet at the end of the corridor, and heating that clattered away most of the night, but I didn't care, I was 19, in London and on expenses! Next problem was nowhere to park…..I did find a space round the back where the bins were, which was fine until the locals blocked my car in with bins! Easily moved, but I had to find another place to park. That other place to park resulted in a parking ticket the next evening….can't claim that back under expenses...or can I?

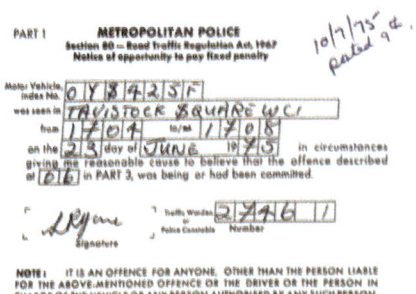

Just the ticket!

Next morning, I headed for the training venue at RR in Hythe Road, Willesden.

No satellite navigation in those days, but my map reading skills were second to none (Aye, right!)

The training venue was old school, in a classroom, roasting hot with the sun beating in, hitting the back of our necks, but the training was most enjoyable. The instructor was a chap called Dennis Robinson, proper chap, accompanied each gesture with a whistle when pointing out what any particular part did, eg "this is the accumulator, and this chap goes here" "whistle", pointing to where it was fitted on the car. Dennis commuted back and forth on a Honda 50cc moped, with one of those old fashioned crash helmets – as I said, a proper chap and real nice guy.

Dennis Robinson Instructor

The training covered mostly current cars, Shadow and T Types, but also covered earlier cars too, as at this point in time, we saw a great deal of Silver Clouds, S Types, R Types and ever earlier through our workshops. The classroom had virtually every part of our cars laid out on a large table….this was great as we could be hands on, stripping each part, finding out how it works, then putting it back together, none of this "just fit a new one", we would overhaul things like height control valves, brake servos, hydraulic accumulators, valve bodies and so on.

I spent an immensely enjoyable 10 days with Dennis and a good bunch of guys from other UK dealerships.

If you cast your mind back to earlier, I had mentioned Billy Connoly....at that point, he was virtually unknown outside of Scotland. We spent most of our lunchtimes out in the car park, doors open on my Sunbeam Stiletto, and Billy blasting out. By the end of the fortnight, I had many (English) fellow classmates belting out "If it wisnae for yer wellies, where would you be"! I think Billy should be giving me royalties for assisting with the launch of his career! I did email him, but as yet he hasn't responded!

I have to admit though, that some of our lunchtimes were also spent playing pool in the local pub...good times.

My Certificate.........

This is to certify

that

Mr. P. Gentles

attended a course at the

Company's School of Instruction

on

Current Production Cars

from **23.6.75** *to* **4.7.75**

on behalf of

Appleyard (Glasgow) Ltd.

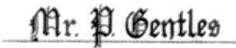

for Rolls-Royce Motors Limited

Principal:

I learned an awful lot on that course, the start of many courses, dealer launches, meetings, trips and awards. 48 years is a long time to be with one Marque (Well two, R-R & B)...Wish I'd made it to the half century, but times change, not always for the better......

One course in London worth a mention was the time Willie Curry and myself were sent for a three day course, the content of which I cannot remember. Our friend and colleague Jimmy McGuinness was due to come to London the same day we were meant to leave. We decided that we would stay on an extra night and all three of us would go down Soho. Off we duly went, and went into a striptease club, as one does. What a dump! It ended up with just the three of us in the audience, and we ended up blethering to the lady on stage. It was a bad move staying the extra night without authority, big John Findlay tore us a new arsehole when we got back to work! Enough about London, the training was soon to be relocated in the Crewe factory.

Her Majesty the queen was paying a royal visit to Scotland as part of her Silver jubilee celebrations. We got word that one of the door locks on her Rolls-Royce was acting up, which would never do! Myself and Mike went to the secure police garage where the car was stored in readiness. Security was understandably very high, but somehow they let us in! We fixed the fault with the lock, and feeling rather chuffed with ourselves, headed back to Maxwell Park. This was to be the first of two times I was close to where HRH had parked her arse, the next time would be many years later, on the royal yacht Britannia, more of which later on.

I reckon her Majesty's visit was on the 17th of May, 1977..... the procession was to drive along Titwood road, which was just at the rear of the garage complex. We were allowed some time off to watch the procession, as it would be unlikely that any of us would get another chance to see her Majesty, unless of course if I were to receive a knighthood, in which case I'd meet her face to face, and I could tell her that it was myself and Mike who fixed her door lock – do you get knighted for things like that? Seems anyone can get a knighthood these days (Lewis Hamilton?), so why not me? Arise Sir Peter – has a nice ring to it! Anyway, I digress...

The whole workforce made their way up to the end of the garage, where there was a railway embankment, where we all sat to watch Liz go by in The Rolls-Royce which we had fixed – did I mention that we had fixed it?

We all then went back to work, and whether one is a royalist or not, I don't think there was anyone there that didn't return with a sense of pride and excitement at seeing her Majesty.

I did work on the side most Saturdays, in a bodyshop belonging to Jackie Collins, a friend of my dads. The bodyshop was called John R Collins Ltd, in Mauchline Street, and I would do most of the mechanical stripping and rebuilding of accident damaged vehicles. It was a job I didn't relish much, but the money was good, and there were a few perks, for example they repainted a V12 Jaguar I had, and also my Rover 3500 at real "mates rates"!

My very first homer was fitting a new exhaust to a Morris Minor 1000, which my pal Brian and I received the princely sum of £3.00 (Allegedly). We promptly spent it on a curry, which was going to be a common occurrence! My first homer on a RR/B was assisting Barry Kilgour, a pal and fellow colleague to fit two rear shock absorbers to a Bentley T1, registration number 3DWC. It belonged to a chap called Jack Lapin, and Jack would be a loyal customer for me until his passing. We did it at Barry's garage at his house. This gave me a taste of the *earnings that could be achieved.

*For the benefit of the Inland Revenue, we never received monetary payment, only the occasional pint from friends!

Doing homers on RR and Bentley cars was a strict no-no, if caught would lead to disciplinary action, maybe even dismissal, so we had to be very careful. We would buy the parts from the stores, the storeman was sworn to secrecy, and smuggle the parts out. I remember stuffing two shock absorbers down the legs of my overalls, and had to walk across the lane from the parts department, by the directors office, and into our workshop. All was going well until one of the shockers slipped and poked out the leg of my overalls. In an effort to retrieve it, the other one slipped out the other leg! All this in front of a directors office. He couldn't have been looking, as I got away with it by the skin of my teeth!

I remember doing some work on a travel agents Rolls-Royce Corniche, and when I dropped the car back to him to get payment, he offered me a choice. From memory, he owed me something like £170.00, which he held in his hand, or he said myself and my girlfriend could have a two week holiday in Lloret de Mar.

This was around 1975 or so, when a holiday there was considerably more than the *£170, so a no-brainer really, my first holiday abroad!

Again for the benefit of the Inland Revenue, I declared this in my annual tax return!

I had a lock up at the back of Mellor and Thomsons garage in Crossmyloof, where most of my time outwith work was spent, either doing homers or tinkering with my own cars, boats, and motorcycles. There was a lot of like minded individuals with lock ups there, and I made some good friends, and often just on the spur of the moment, jumping on our motorbikes and heading to Oban for chips or pizza... great times.

One day, during torrential rain, which I know is pretty unheard of in Scotland, the drains at the lock ups overflowed, causing a massive oil slick, as persons or persons unknown had been disposing of waste oil down the drains! (Not me M'Lud!)
The director from Mellor and Thomsons was not at all pleased, and vowed to catch the culprit or culprits.

There were no toilet facilities at the lock ups, so we used an empty gallon can when required. We would go home if anything other than a pee was required. One day, the aforesaid mentioned director came running down, and accused me of pouring oil down the drain. He snatched the guilty can from me, sniffed it, and ran his finger round the edge. "That's the can we do the toilet in" I sniggered, at which point, he launched the can away, and buggered off in a right hissy fit. We had no more bother after that.

There was no mains power, so we had a system of car batteries and lamps if we had to work at night, which we often did, I recall doing an "all-nighter" to get a car finished. I was nothing to us, being considerably younger then.

We made a good additional living those days, and the lock up was only given up when Jimmy and I started our own company, RRS (Glasgow) Limited, more of which later.

In those days I had it all, bikes, cars, and boats…..I spent more on fuel than most people earned!

Appleyard was giving up the Rolls-Royce franchise, it was getting taken on by Stanley Gauld, so a clear out was required. A skip was hired and put in the yard. It was a sin, but there were thousands of pounds worth of obsolete parts, which today would be very much in demand.
Mike Jarvie would not be going with us, instead starting his own business, M B Jarvie Ltd along with Alistair Cairns. Mike spent most of his time, actually in the skip, taking whatever parts he could use. The skip became known as "Mikes Office", and if anyone was looking for him, he could be found "in his office!"

The next chapter will see us in Gaulds of Glasgow, on the Mosspark Boulevard…

Chapter Four - The Gaulds of Glasgow years

Appleyard had had enough and were giving up the RR & B franchise round about 1980. The main contender was Stanley Gauld, who owned Gaulds of Stewarton, a Ford dealership. Stanley was a Rolls-Royce owner himself, and along with his friend Fraser Anderson, who was the Appleyard RR/B sales manager, they were granted (if that's the word) the Rolls-Royce and Bentley franchise for the West of Scotland. The premises were to be the old Mellor and Thompson garage at the end of Mosspark Boulevard, and the place was soon kitted out with all new equipment and we were back in business. Stanley had interviewed all the staff before making the decision to streamline the new operation, and some didn't transfer to the new place. Mike Jarvie and Alistair Cairns were two of the staff not going, but they decided to start up their own business, firstly just along from Charing Cross, then a move to the current premises in Stanley Street, Kinning Park, where the company M B Jarvie is still going strong.

John Findlay was still the service manager, and I was the chargehand technician. Fraser Anderson sales director, and Russell Forsyth and Mel Brown were sales executives. This was the first time I had met Russell.

Mel Brown and Bob Martin in the showroom at 582 Mosspark Mosspark Boulevard

I had just been charged for going through a red light (I still deny it to this day) and under the totting up process, I was due a ban. Stanley (STG) came up to court with me, and spoke up for me and the business, saying that my licence was crucial to his new business, as I was the chief road tester. I didn't get banned, just a hefty fine. I'll always be grateful to STG for that.

In those days, new cars were collected at the factory in Crewe, and driven back to the dealership. I remember getting the train to Crewe, and getting picked up at the station and taken to the factory. Security was nothing like it is now, all you needed was a letter from the dealership, and you could drive away in a new car! I remember you had to wait in a waiting room, while the paperwork was sorted out. This was long before the factory had a total facelift.

One New Years Eve, we had a customer insisting on getting his new Silver Spirit (in Light Ocean Blue as they all seemed to be in that era, or Cotswold Beige) before midnight, so he could drive the car out of his garage on the First of January. No names here, but he wasn't the sort of guy you could say no to. He did own a carpet store in Maryhill, and is now no longer with us.

I collected the car at the factory, and drove it back without incident, that is until I was half a mile from the dealership, and a lady driving a Ford Fiesta pulled out from the inside lane, and hit the side of the Spirit. Names and details exchanged, but my main concern was to get the car back so the damage could be fixed. On closer inspection, there was only a very slight nick on the left front wheel arch, and a slight "ding" on the left front wheel trim. I carried out the pre-delivery inspection on the car, touched up the wheel arch, and changed the wheel trim to the opposite side on the rear. This was really just to give us some breathing space, and not wanting to disappoint the owner, we duly delivered the car. The plan was to get it back at a later date and get it repaired, but it was never noticed, so It was decided to let sleeping dogs lie!

There was one time myself and Willie Curry had delivered a car to it's owner, and on our way back, Willie was driving the bosses brand new Ford Fiesta (no more Marinas, we were onto Fords now!), and we were sitting at the lights on Paisley Road West, Willie was ready to go, handbrake off, foot on the clutch ready for the lights to change. I secretly pulled the handbrake on, unbeknown to Willie. The lights changed, Willie took off and immediately stalled it! A Volvo then rammed right into the back of us! In the words of Willie "I was sure I'd left the handbrake off!" or expletives to that affect!

I never admitted it until several years later, and he was working for me, then we had a good laugh about it. The Volvo, being a Volvo was undamaged, but the Fiesta needed slightly more!

This chapter would not be the same without mentioning Ann McGee, who was the cleaner. Lovely lady, who took it upon herself to bring in a gas cooker hob, and made everyone rolls and sausage every day, and only charged us what it cost her. Saved us going to the shops and saved us money.
I still remember how good they tasted…...

Stanley had his Ford dealership in Stewarton, Ayrshire, which had a full body and paintwork operation. Any paintwork we had in Glasgow had to be sent there for completion, not ideal. I helped out where I could with paintwork given our very limited facilities.

Yours truly repainting a Silver Shadow in Caribbean Blue

Please note the "state of the art" facilities!

It was decided to install our own paintwork facility in the rear workshop. A new paint booth was installed, and Billy Hunter was headhunted to organise that side of the business as a hands-on painter. Billy was a very good painter.

My first wife at the time had a mini, and I decided for her birthday, I would give her car a new lease of life, I took one of my weeks holiday, and set about the task. I stripped it, and welded all the body seams (called de-seaming), which, for anyone who knows the original Mini, involved getting rid of all the unsightly gutters and seams. Big job, but eventually finished, Billy Hunter kindly repainted it in BMW red, to match my BMW 320 I had at the time. It looked stunning. I fitted Wood and Picket dash and nudge bars, Woolfrace wheels and wheel arch extensions to set the whole thing off.

Matching cars

Early on in the Silver Spirit/Mulsanne era, there was found to be wind noises and vibrations coming from the door frames at speed. This was due to a design mistake, later to be sorted out on production, but in the meantime, all the original cars had to be retrospectively repaired. This was a fairly major undertaking, and myself and Jim McGuinness were trained to do the necessary work. We bought a TIG (Tungsten Inert Gas) welder, as the recall consisted of removing all four window frames, and welding stainless steel fillet plates to the front and rear of the frames. As some of the welding would be seen, it was to be ground flat, sanded, and polished to a mirror finish. I used to etch my name on the unseen parts of the repair, as I was proud of the finished repairs.

The factory allowed sixteen man hours for each car, and after a few, I could manage it in eight, earning me a substantial bonus.

In their wisdom, the factory decided that all Silver Shadows and derivatives, along with early Spirits had to be recalled for an issue with the boot lock. It was discovered that if the rear edge of the boot lid was pushed in, the boot would spring open. The new lock was of a different design, which did not allow this to happen.

I wish I had a pound for every owner that wanted compensated for "the golf clubs" or "other valuables" that had got stolen over the years due to this fault! Every single car going back to the introduction of Shadow had to be done. Each customer had to be contacted, long before the age of computer assistance, so you can imagine the size of the task.

We won the RR and Bentley dealer of the year in 1982, and Stanley treated us all to lunch in the workshop, setting up a long table, complete with silver service.

Left to Right:
Big John Findlay
Myself, Peter Gentles
Alistair Reid
(Rolls-Royce area manager)

Both Big John and Alistair
have sadly passed away RIP

Fraser Anderson on the left,
with Bernard Preston from
Rolls-Royce.

Above, Left to Right:

Two apprentices (their names escape me)
Bob Martin (Administrator)
Mellis T Brown (Sales)
Stanley T Gauld (Owner)
Billy Hunter (Paintshop)
Fraser Anderson
Myself (Peter Gentles)
Bernard Preston (Director of RR)
Gordon Adam (Auto Electrician) hiding
Jimmy McGuinness (Mate)
Jeff Cowell, big wig from RR
Steph McBride (Apprentice)
Colin Blakey (Apprentice)
Alistair Reid (RR area manager)
Donald Cameron (Parts Manager)
And last but not least, Big John Findlay

Fraser Anderson and Stanley Gauld decided on a parting of the ways, Fraser leaving to do his own thing, initially selling Rolls-Royce and Bentley cars (I later bought my Silver Cloud 1 from him), and then opening a Subaru dealership in Stirling, more of which later.

Stanley Gauld had brought in a new director, Martin Shaw, a yuppie with an expensive suit and shiny shoes.

One day, I was lying under a Silver Shadow, fitting new liners and pistons, not an easy job, and one requiring a lot of care and concentration. Martin Shaw stuck his head under the car and told me to road test a Jaguar XJS, at which point I politely refused, explaining that I was in the middle of a crucial procedure, and he would need to wait. Not acceptable to him, one word led to another, and I told him to shove the Jaguar up his arse! That earned me a disciplinary letter, the one and only one I ever got in any of my 48 years.

I mentioned fitting liners and pistons to a Shadow. This came about because a car we had sold, every now and then would belch out clouds of smoke from the exhaust.

The car was covered by the used car warranty, so when it first appeared, big John decided it must be the valve stem oil seals. These were replaced and the car tested. Still the same fault, but to cut a long story short (too late!) it was agreed with the warranty company to replace all eight pistons and cylinder liners. Once I'd done all that (no small task) I was asked to test the car for my first time, (always previously carried out by big John).

The car was exactly the same, but I caught a whiff of the smoke, and it wasn't engine oil, more like transmission fluid. I went back into the workshop for further checking. Now, without getting too technical (too late!), the up and down gearchanges are to a certain extent partly governed by a suction operated modulator valve. This takes its suction from the inlet manifold, so I disconnected the suction pipe, and attached a length of hose to the valve. I sucked it and got a mouth full of transmission fluid!

Fault found, the rubber diaphragm in the valve had split. I whipped a valve off an old gearbox, which took all of ten minutes, tested the car - perfect! All that for a ten minute job.

I occasionally came across the same car, still with the same owner, and the engine is still like new.

The Service manager, John Findlay, decided not to pursue his career with Gaulds of Glasgow, and went to run a new Nissan dealership in Pollokshaws, Glasgow. It was owned by a good friend of his, hence the change. Martin Shaw brought in one of his old team from Hamilton Brothers Fiat as service manager. I've got to admit, I threw the teddy out the pram to a certain extent, as I reckon that job should have been mine. Apparently I was too valuable as a mechanic on the workshop floor. The rot was starting to set in, and I must admit to being a balshy bugger, not making it easy for either of the two new guys.

Myself and my mate Jimmy had been doing "homers" (home jobs, or foreigners) for a good while,
and thought this was the right time to move on, starting our own garage repair operation. The seed was sown! We surely had enough customers to hit the ground running?
We had a friend who worked in Rolls-Royce Aero Engine division in Hillington, and in the past, he had machined various tools and items for us if we needed something unique. We made and arrangement for us to sneak to him some of the special tools, he would copy them and we would return the original. One day, someone spotted us sneaking a tool into the boot of a car, and reported us to Martin Shaw. I have to this day, my thoughts on who reported us, but unable to substantiate it.
We were called into the workshop office, where we were accused of stealing the tool, and I admitted we were only borrowing it to have a copy made. I should have lied, but I came clean and admitted Jimmy and myself were going out on our own.
We were told to get back to work. Later that day, I was dismissed, whereas Jimmy was kept on, why? Because seemingly I was the "mastermind" behind this incident, but, truth be told, Jimmy was in the middle of a big hydraulic contamination repair which only Jimmy could have finished.
Anyway, Jimmy handed in his notice, and left shortly afterwards...RRS (Glasgow) Ltd was born. We were visited by the police, and all they found was a pressure gauge that was mine. They held onto it for "evidence", and subsequently I got it returned.
I have regrets about the way I handled this, and looking back, would things have been any different?
You bet your life!

Chapter Five – The RRS Glasgow Limited Years

In 1985, I left Gaulds of Glasgow, left being the nice way of putting it!

I had a week to set up a new company, RRS (Glasgow) Ltd, which was conducting business in Garrioch Road Maryhill. My good friend, Jim McGuinness and I were directors in the new venture, having put in £300.00 each to get us started. I had organised to rent the premises from Jim Watt MBE, as it was part of his tyre fitting business. Jim used to be pretty big in the rally side of things, having a mobile unit run by my mate John Dunbar, which attended most UK rallies, supplying and fitting tyres, but he had decided to give that up, which left some space that we could rent. (John was also my best man at my first wedding)

Things were pretty basic to start with, we built an office, and bought a second hand desk.....we were directors in our own business! Wow!

The name RRS was initials for Rolls-Royce Service, as we couldn't use the full title due to copyright. If you had a Range Rover or Reliant Robin, we would tell you that's what RRS stood for too!

Jimmy and I had quite a customer base from all the homers we used to do, but transferring customers we had doing homers did not quite equate to a full weeks work for both of us, as we soon found out....we were skint! Some six or so months down the line, I bought Jimmy out, and he got himself a job with our old boss, John Findlay. I had made a commitment to keep going, so keep going I did. Jimmy always helped me out if I had a big or two-man job in.

Around that time, my old boss and friend Fraser Anderson had started up a Subaru Dealership in Dripp Road, Stirling. He asked me to run the aftersales side of it, which I thought long and hard about, eventually declining as I had made a commitment to keep RRS going. I did interview a chap called Fraser Murray to fill the new role with Fraser Anderson, which he took on admirably for many years.

I had heard great things about the Harvey Bailey handling kit for Silver Shadow and Bentley T. I enquired with them directly with a view to gaining the agency for Scotland. Rhoddy Harvey Bailey and one of his colleagues brought up one of their modified Silver Shadows for me to test. I did, and got done for speeding along the Great Western Road – not a great start. What a difference the kit made to the Shadow though, not quite turning it into a sports car, but certainly did away with a great deal of the "wallowing" associated with the Shadow.

The down side was they wanted me to keep three kits in stock at £2500 each, not something I could afford at that time, particularly having to pay a speeding fine! Lol

We shook hands and parted company, but it had been worth a try.

My marital home in Beith, Ayrshire went as security to the bank, giving me the capital to start up a wedding car business. I bought, for the princely sum of £10,250, a 1958 Rolls-Royce Silver Cloud in Shell Grey, with a red interior. I knew the car, as we had been maintaining it for quite some time, both now, and previously. The first owner of the car was Sir Thomas Sopwith, a pioneer aviator, and largely responsible for the Sopwith Camel, which played a major part in World War One. He was also a famous yachtsman, almost winning the Americas cup in 1934. Anyway, he was the first owner. I also bought a 200E Mercedes, which I myself, personally, repainted in Shell Grey to match the RR. I also bought a 280SE Mercedes, my wedding fleet was complete.

The fleet, with some of the other cars I borrowed on a regular basis

Jim Watt MBE had also started a wedding business with a Honey Gold Silver Shadow 2 which I had arranged for him with Fraser Anderson. His wife Margaret would drive it at weddings, along with the two Mercedes they had. We worked well together, backing each other up, and I used to be very busy with trade weddings, as I had pictures of my Silver Cloud in a few wedding shops.

Anyway, moving on, Jim Watt had decided to sell the garage, to be made into housing, as that was a more profitable move. I sourced a 5,600 square foot unit in Hillington Industrial Estate, big move, meant taking on more staff, and I decided to move into paint and body repairs, restoration, and MOT testing, along with the usual servicing and repairs. I signed a lease with the Scottish Development Agency (SDA), to be reviewed in 5 years. I approached Shell Oil, as at that time, they would fund workshop equipment, as long as I purchased all workshop oils and fluids from them. Seemed like a good idea at the time.

We were to become a Gemini Service Centre, Gemini being the brand name of Shells Elite motor oil (and most expensive!).

Now a Gemini Service Centre.

*Myself and Ken McNab
from Shell oils making it official.*

*Same scene with the team Left to Right
Nancy (Book keeper)
Karen (Wife and fellow director)
Blair Beck (Bodyshop foreman)
Canny Mind! (Apprentice)
Ronnie Clelland (Apprentice)
Willie Currie (Mechanic)
James Crewes (Apprentice)*

In retrospect, I should perhaps have walked before I ran, but I wanted to be the best, so embarked on a spending spree, new ramps, MOT station, spray paint booth, all on funding from Shell. This meant I had a massive target of oil to sell, but hey, I could do it, or so I thought. Any shortfall in oil target meant I had to pay the interest on what was basically a loan, sometimes amounting to a substantial amount of money.

The wedding hire business was ticking over, but when I was approached to sell the Rolls-Royce, I couldn't really refuse, as it meant a profit of over sixteen thousand pounds, which would come in very handy.
Sadly, the car was sold, but I still keep in touch with the lad that bought it, and he still has it some 28 years later.

On the subject of my Silver Cloud, I used an image of it to grace my company letterheads and compliments slips. Out of the blue I got a letter from the legal department of Rolls-Royce, stating that I was infringing their copyright on the trademark radiator shell by using a picture of my own car! I was to stop using them forthwith or they would take legal proceedings. To hell with them I thought, it's my car and I'll put a picture on if I want. I ignored them and heard no more about it!

While on the subject of letters, around the time of the Gulf War early 1991, Ronnie Clelland, one of my apprentices came to me to say he had been accepted for the Royal Navy, with a starting date of some 3 months hence. He asked if he could stay on until then, to which I agreed, as he had been honest with me, and he was a great wee worker. Got to admit I'd be sorry to see him go.
I hatched a plan to get him with a hoax, cruel I know, but seemed like a laugh at the time. I had taken a copy of his navy acceptance letter, and typed up a letter using the name of the officer that had written to him. Briefly, the letter told him that due to the escalation of hostilities in the Gulf War, his starting date was brought forward. He was to meet up with other recruits at George Square a week on Sunday at 06.00 hours, where he would be taken to Faslane naval base, to board HM submarine Dreadnought, and immediately embark on two week intensive attack and destroy training course.
In my previous conversation with Ronnie, I found out that the one thing he was afraid of was submarines!

I forged the officers signature, and put the letter in an envelope, which I used for sending in my PAYE, and looked official with government markings. Posted it and though no more about until a few days later, when Ronnies father appeared at my office door having taken a taxi from his home. He was clutching his chest with one hand, and my letter in the other! Shit! "My boy, my boy, they've called up my boy to fight in the war" he gasped! "Go and show the letter to the foreman" I said, just to give me some thinking time, or should I just run away?

I thought it best to just come clean and suffer the consequences. He took it pretty well, more out of relief that his boy hadn't been called up. I refunded his taxi cost and we had a bit of a laugh about it.

Talk about a prank backfiring! I had learned my lesson....or had I?

I always bought my RR parts from Gaulds, my previous employer. One day they called me up, would I be interested in making an offer for their obsolete parts stock, which was getting written off for year end. I offered £500 and got the parts. Two crates of parts were delivered, and when I opened them, to my delight there were four RR Silver Spirit radiator shells, which were valued about £2k each! Result! The rest of the parts were still very useful, mostly for older cars, which I specialised in.

I bought and sold a few Rolls-Royce cars, the profit from these was the icing on the cake, but I won't go into each one individually, suffice to say, they were quite lucrative.

I said I wouldn't go into each one, but this one was a belter! While I was still in Garrioch Road, I got a phone call from a wedding business in Ayrshire. When I say wedding business, the guy owned a 1982 Silver Spirit and did weddings on the side! He was in a panic, the car would not move, and he had a wedding the next day. I jumped into my car, and armed with some tools, headed to Ayr. The fault was with the electronic gear actuator, which wouldn't allow any gear selection. Nothing could be done until I could source the parts required. He pleaded with me, and I agreed the only way was to manually move the gearbox into drive, but the danger was it would start in gear, and not much in the way of brakes until the engine was run. Some two weeks later, I got a call saying that he had lent the car to a mate, but forgot to inform him of the gearchange issue! The car had started on full choke, in drive, no brakes, and went straight through a wall! No insurance.....

The car was transported to me for assessment, which turned out to be pretty serious, front chassis leg bent and the drivers wing destroyed, along with numerous other damages.

Alarm bells were ringing, so I insisted on £3,000 "up front" money before repairs were commenced.

Car was stripped, engine and subframe removed and new chassis leg and wing replaced. I then got a visit from the customer, saying he now wanted the car colour changed from Light Ocean Blue to White. Another deposit of £2,500 was obtained. Some three years later, after numerous attempts to contact the customer, I was reluctant to go any further with repairs. We had moved over to the unit in Hillington by this time, and the car was taking up valuable space. (the doors were all off and the engine was still out)

I checked and found the car was still on finance, so, unable to get the owner, a cunning plot was hatched. A good friend of mine contacted the finance company, told them where the car was, and offered to buy it for £8,000. They sent out an assessor, who found the car in it's sorry state. His offer to buy was accepted, and I bought the car with £250 "finders fee" to my mate.

I decided that white was not the colour, so the car was refinished in Royal Blue Metallic. The car was completed and looked amazing. It was sitting in my yard, fortunately with no number plates, when who should arrive but the "owner"! Said he had been "out the country" for three years, and was here to collect his car!

"Bad news" I replied, "the finance company had repossessed the car, and was no longer here." We were standing right beside the car as our conversation took place….He said leave it with him, and he will sort it out with the finance company. I never saw him again….luckily!

I sold the car for £26,500, and took back a lovely Peacock Blue Shadow in part exchange. Wish I had deals like that every month!

Our main business over and above the day to day service, repairs and MOT's was restoration of classic cars, mainly Rolls-Royce and Bentley.

One car, the oldest we ever worked on, was a Darracq, from about 1910 I reckon, which we MOT'd sympathetically ever year.

The owner was Dr Meek, who also had a Silver Mink Silver Shadow which we also looked after.

Dr Meek and his Silver Shadow are long since gone, but the Darracq is still in the family

It wouldn't be right if I didn't mention the help I got from my dad, being retired, he worked almost every day with me, going for parts, banking, general things about the garage. He always liked to be busy. He wouldn't accept any payment, but we always looked after his car and filled the tank with fuel for him.

I remember he had a wee Mazda 323 which was showing it's age. My dad was in hospital at the time (one of many times) so we took the opportunity to repair, repaint and overhaul his wee car while he was incapacitated. His face was a joy when we surprised him with the car looking like new when he got out of hospital.

One time, several years previously, I got a phone call from the manager of a large shop in Finnieston. He thought my dad had a heart attack and could I come over ASAP as dad wouldn't let him call an ambulance! I jumped in my Mercedes and was soon there. Dad was sitting there, and seemed to be a bit better. I put him in my car and started to take him to hospital, better safe than sorry. While we were sitting at traffic lights on the Broomielaw, dad started clutching his chest....

There were two motorcycle cops a couple of cars in front of us, I ran up to them and asked if they could radio ahead to the Victoria Infirmary, so they would be ready to deal with dad right away.

The cop said, and I'll always remember his words, "we'll do better than that sir, follow us!"

They speed off, leapfrogging at junctions, through red lights, stopping traffic, with me in my Mercedes doing what seemed like 90mph along Victoria Road. We soon got to the hospital, and a team were waiting outside for us. I never got the chance to thank the cops, but I managed a "Thumbs up" as I followed dad into A & E. Thanks guys, whoever you were.....

Dad hadn't had a heart attack as it turned out, it was a severe angina attack which has very similar symptoms. He soon recovered, and later had an angioplasty operation, which made him a new man. He was able to watch the operation on a monitor, and he had nothing but praise for the medical team and the Victoria.

Anyway.....I digress.....

General view looking down the workshop…..

Mostly RR and Bentley, but a Healey 3000, and an Aston DB5 Volante visible in the top left corner, beside the Silver Dawn I went to Germany to inspect. A BMW is on the ramp for an MOT test.

Jaguar V12 E-Type before

And after

Austin Healey 3000 before...

Austin Healey 3000 after...

5 years soon went by, the business had it's ups and downs, but we had a great name and did a great deal of local business. A severe blow came after the 5 year lease was up, the SDA (Scottish Development Agency) from whom I had leased the building had sold off to the private sector, and now they were to more than double the rent! Hillington had moved upmarket from "Hillington Industrial Estate" to "Hillington Business Park". I kind of lost heart in the business, and lost focus.

At this time, my painter and panelbeater was off on fairly long term sick. I was paying him full wages, on the advice of my accountants, which turned out to be incorrect information. They admitted their mistake, and offered their services free for the following year. Not much help at this point in time.

One of the paint manufacturing reps, Jimmy Duncan stepped in to help, coming in most evenings to do my paintwork, essentially bailing me out the shite.

By this time, our house in Beith, I regret had been sold and we were living seventeen stories up in a tower block in Pollokshaws, in one of the less desirable areas of Glasgow. Having recently passed through it, it is now a different place, the old tower blocks have been demolished, and lovely new housing in their place.

I came out one morning to find my Ford XR3i Cabriolet was vandalised, tyres and hood slashed, paintwork scored - I had to get out of there!

In the preceding year, I had spent some £47,500 on RR and Bentley parts, from the then only dealer in Scotland, Murray Motor Company in Edinburgh. I had a temporary cash flow issue, and had asked them for a few weeks extra to settle my monthly account. Next I got a call from Alex in their parts department saying that the owner of Murrays, Mr John Martin, wanted to come across and see me. Hmm, I owed them £1400, was this something the owner wanted personally to deal with? Obviously I agreed, and a few days later, John Martin came over with an entourage, including his managing director Gordon Nisbet and his aftersales manager Gary Bagley.....overkill I thought.

We had a long chat, and I showed them around, introducing them to my team. Then came the surprise!

John Martin offered me a job, setting up a new Rolls-Royce, Bentley, Aston Martin and Lotus dealership in the city centre....I had to think long and hard with this one!

The pro's were a regular salary, company car, and less hours, the con's being I wasn't my own boss, working for an employer again.

I decided to accept their offer, which included taking with me a few of my team. After advice from my accountant, the best way forward would be to put the company into liquidation, as the sale value would be nil, other than the goodwill, which I was taking with me to Murray Motors.

It was a sad, sad day, I watched as all my equipment was auctioned off, but I was to see my MOT ramp and station again, as John Martin bought it to install in one of his branches.

The end of an era....onwards and hopefully upwards.........

Chapter Six – The Murray Motor Company Years

Well, here I was, my first day with Murray Motor Company. I was to spend a fortnight at the Rolls-Royce and Bentley dealership in Edinburgh, just to ease into their ways of working, and to learn some of the systems.

I met John Martin, the chairman that morning, who, as previously mentioned had spent a fair bit of time with me in RRS, and we were on friendly first name terms. I said "good morning John", and he frowned and said angrily "It's MR MARTIN!" and I thought to myself, fuck….have I made the right move coming here!

However, I soon settled down, and the thought of setting up the new dealership in Charing Cross back in my home city of Glasgow and the challenge facing me became quite exciting. Initially we would have Rolls-Royce, Bentley, Aston Martin and Lotus, in what was a fairly tight city centre location.

We soon had the place up and running, Russell Forsyth in sales, and myself in the aftersales. I was running the parts department as well as the workshop, but once we became busier, things would change. This was also my first experience of computers, never having used them in RRS, but soon picked it up. The computers had pretty basic programmes, which was fine, nothing like the complex systems in use today.

We put on a Bentley Eight as a courtesy car, which was good, meant I could use if it wasn't out on loan!

We subsequently changed it for a Lexus LS300, which was also a fine car.

I organised what we would call a service week or clinic, which involved inviting customers in, where, along with two factory engineers, we would carry out an inspection and road test, whereupon the customer would be sat down and the engineer from the factory along with myself, would go over any concerns or issues that were highlighted during the inspection.

This was a lot of work, and would involve preparing estimates for any work required. It would usually work out quite lucrative in the longer term.

During this week, was our first real involvement with Angus Boyd, the owner of Mitchells restaurant just a few doors along from us in North Street. It was arranged that if a customer came in the morning, while his or her car was inspected, we would call Angus, and he would send down whatever the customer wanted for breakfast.

Same for lunchtime, and later on for afternoon tea. Mitchells food was superb, and Angus and I built up a friendship that lasts to this day, although he now concentrates on his restaurant in Carmunnock, on the outskirts of Glasgow.

One customer sticks out here, cannot for the life of me remember his name, nor would I want to remember. He brought in possibly the worst example of a Silver Shadow I have encountered. He was a farmer, and brought with him his "mechanic" both of whom looked as if they had just serviced a tractor, and rolled about in the mud while doing so. The pair sat down in our showroom, at a table resplendent with a pristine white tablecloth, and promptly ordered lobster from the lunch menu.
In retrospect, I should have chased them. The car was a pile of junk, with some four pages of faults, all of which had to be estimated. What a waste of time, never saw him again, he didn't even buy the parts from us!
The only good thing was at the end of a hard week, we had a fantastic night out at Mitchells, to thank the guys from the factory.

A young motley crew at Mitchells after a hard week....

Myself second back on left in the black shirt...

Around this time, I had parted from my wife, shortly to be divorced, but unusually, I had custody of my two kids, Roy and Stephanie. Always looking for something different to entertain them, particularly at weekends, I took them to a newly opened magic shop in the High Street in Glasgow. This shop was great, in as much as the staff were all either professional or amateur magicians. If you expressed interest in a trick, they would perform the trick for you, and if you liked it then bought it, they would take you round the side and show you how it was done.
This made a pleasant change from other shops, where you bought a trick then you were left to your own devices.

One of the staff, Alan, asked if I would be interested in a magic course he was running. Alan, or Al Dee as he was known proffessionaly, signed me up for an eight week beginners course, followed by an eight week advanced course. For both final tests, I had to perform what I'd learnt in front of an audience. I still have my certificates which I treasure.

I did a magic show for one of Stephanie's birthday parties, and also performed at a few Bentley meetings. One time in a hotel, I did an act in front of about forty delegates, the hotel staff scurrying about trying at find playing cards and props for the act. What a laugh we had. Anyway, again I digress...

I would often take the factory reps out for dinner at their visits, so decided to do something a bit different, so I got a corporate membership from the Cue Club, a snooker hall not far from the dealership at Charing Cross.
This was the time I met a character called Terry Allman, who was the RR and Bentley area service manager (ASM). I say character, because at the time, I lived in Dumbarton, and Terry at his monthly visit would book into the hotel next to my house. We would have dinner there, play pool and get pished! One night, he did try and chat up my first wife!
Terry changed his role, and we briefly got a new ASM, a lad called Dave Hayter, then after him we had Nigel Gelsthorpe, or the Winsford Warrior as he was known in the factory. Nigel and I still keep in touch. I call him "Mr Gleesthorpe" which is a standing joke from when we met an Asian customer who couldn't quite pronounce Gelsthorpe.

I still have the Cue Club membership, and really, up until the Covid Pandemic, myself and three pals, Ian, Stevie and Russell would go there every Tuesday evening.

One time, some years later when working for Douglas Park, I was returning home, sitting, waiting on the lights changing, and singing along to "Bangra Nights" (The theme tune to a Peugeot Television advert you may remember) I was in a Skoda Octavia VRS, which I had chipped to 225 brake horse power, anyway, I digress. The CD was at full volume, window open and I was rocking! I felt, however that someone was watching me, turned to my right and there was a Mercedes with four Asian guys, looking daggers at me, no doubt thinking I was taking the piss, which of course, I wasn't!

I was glad of that 225bhp when the lights changed and I was off!

It was during my time with Murrays, I met Marti Pellow of Wet Wet Wet. The group were staying at an exclusive hotel, namely "One Devonshire Gardens", and would get various cars, including Aston Martins, delivered for them to try. None of them ever bought anything though.

I did get an autograph for each of my kids, and when I showed them, they said "who?", having never heard of the group. I did get three VIP tickets for the gig, which the kids slept through the whole performance, only coming to life when we went backstage after the show, where there was a huge buffet, and the kids had a field day. You would think I never fed them!

Marti Pellow would surface again at Parks, and bought a Range Rover from our Ayr branch. I believe he did sing at one of Douglas Parks birthday celebrations.

I once had a dream about Marti Pellow, it was my first "Wet Wet Wet" dream! Taxi for Peter!

One Saturday morning, when I was opening up, I notice something strange under the arch which was the access to the rear of the garage. On closer inspection, it turned out to be a pile of human faeces (a jobby), and a pair of underpants which the previous owner of the jobby had used to clean him (or her)self. Yuk! Armed with a suitably long pair of pliers,

I heaved the pants behind a wall. The rain would wash the jobby away, so that was that. The underpants became affectionately known as "the tramps pants", the relevance of this will become clear shortly.

We had managed to "borrow" a technician from Edinburgh, a great guy called Norman J McKenzie, until I had recruited my own team. Norman had the use of a Ford Sierra estate to travel back and forth from Edinburgh to Glasgow, and when the time came to return to his post in Edinburgh, he brought the car into the workshop to load up all his tools. I noticed a camera on the back seat, so I had an idea for some mischief! I sneaked the camera, and took it into the toilet, and I took a photo of a little jobby which was floating in the pan... it may or may not have been me that put it there, ok, ok, it was me! Anyway, jobby picture taken, and camera secretly placed back in the car.
I found out several days later that it wasn't Normans camera, but belonged to his, at that time, future mother in law! Oops!

This started a light hearted feud between Norrie and myself, admittedly at a distance of around 42.2 miles, that being the distance between the Glasgow and Edinburgh branches of Murray Motor company.

There was a parts van delivery system in operation, which doubled as our method of internal mail delivery from Head Office in Edinburgh.
One day, I received a jiffy bag addressed to me, and inside it was a dead sparrow, which Norman J McKenzie had removed from the grille of an Aston Martin - this was war!

I then procured a rubber condom, and put some liquid soap inside and tied a knot in it. This was duly put in a jiffy bag, and sent through to Mr McKenzie in Edinburgh.
A few days later, another jiffy bag arrived with my name on it. Dreading to think what was inside, I gingerly opened it to find a pound or so of mouldy sausages which Norman had found under the seat of another Aston he was working on. There was hairs and fungus all over them... yuk. Various further exchanges took place, including my sending him a Tampon, which I'd dipped in red paint...

Now, what can beat that? Hmm, back to our old friend, the tramps pants! Using suitably long nose pliers again, I retrieved them from behind the wall. By this time they were crawling with beasties, but no matter, into the jiffy bag they went, and sent to Mr McKenzie. Funny, there were no more instances after that...guess I was victorious, thanks to the tramps pants!

Norman is now doing very well for himself in the United Arab Emirates, nice guy, good luck to him.

Speaking of toilets, one time I was having my morning visit, sitting there minding my own business. I suddenly felt rather unwell, and staggered out into the workshop, where I almost collapsed. Turned out there was a Silver Shadow left running in the workshop, and by some fluke, the exhaust gasses travelled along the back corridor into the toilet...I'd been poisoned! Some fresh air, and I felt a little better, but it was decided to run me home to go to bed. We made it as far as the Kingston bridge, where I violently threw up! I went home and slept, felt great the next morning. In retrospect, probably should have gone to hospital.

It was my fortieth Birthday, and I was working away in my office. This woman police officer came in and ushered me out into the workshop, where the whole team were waiting in a big circle. She just happened to be a "strippergram", and was being videoed! I didn't know where to look, but had a great laugh. I wonder where she is now................

My 40th Birthday present, courtesy of the team!

One time, a gentleman with a 1932 Eight Litre Bentley asked if he could leave the car with us while he went for lunch. No problem, just park it in the workshop. As soon as he left, I put on his goggles and posed at the car....just as he returned as he had forgotten something! Oops, caught. We all found it funny though, he was used to it.

My buddy Jim, and myself
with the goggles.

And the
1932 Bentley Eight Litre

The Aston Martin DB7 had been launched, and I've got to say it was not one of the most reliable cars ever produced. It was arranged for a factory visit to see where the cars were "assembled" and also a visit to the "proper" Aston Martin factory. Looking forward to that one. I was driving to Bloxham with two of my colleagues, Alex Aird from the parts department, and Gary Bagley, who was my boss at the time.

Gary had arranged for us to stay in a Travelodge. I suppose these places serve a purpose, but there was no bar, and the only catering was a vending machine in the hallway.

We were to meet the other delegates at a quaint country hotel for dinner, this place was stunning, just as you would expect from an English country hotel and pub. Why Gary never booked us in there along with the other delegates I'll never know. The food was fabulous, and the first time I had a "Barnsley Chop", a huge double lamb chop. Delicious. Then after some drinks, a drive back to out Travelodge whilst everyone staying at the hotel continued drinking….

The following day, we got a tour of the DB7 production facility at Bloxham, which was just a large industrial unit, with the cars going round on a production line. To my mind, the reason the cars were so unreliable, was partly due to the practice of rotating staff every so often, so one week they could be fitting engines, only to be fitting interiors next time around. I remember watching one guy fitting a propeller shaft, using totally the wrong tools, instead of using a universal joint, his socket kept slipping, accompanied by a great deal of cursing. I just wanted to push him out the way and do it myself!

We then had a tour of the proper factory in Gaydon, where the big cars were made. This was amazing, but like stepping back in time. I particularly remember and aluminium body shell, on a *surface plate, with an old boy sitting on a stool, smoking a pipe. Every so often, he would take a puff of his pipe, and go over to the bodyshell where he would chalk mark another blemish. That was his job….

* A surface plate or table is a perfectly flat sheet of steel, which will enable precise horizontal measurements of the subjects dimensions. These can vary in size depending on the item to be measured.

61

Another antiquated process was when the car bodies were ready, someone would keep an eye out for traffic on the main road, and if clear, the bodyshell would be pushed across the road to the service department, where the power unit etc. would be fitted....

It was a great experience and before leaving for home, we were presented with a green Aston Martin jacket, which I still have. This proved more reliable and waterproof than their cars at the time!

It was decided to have the Chrysler and Jeep franchise added to our other franchises, the plus side was I had a Jeep Cherokee 4 litre as my company car.

I was also in charge of the Chrysler and Jeep press fleet, which meant organising the local motoring journalists in turn to drive the various models for a week or so. Our task was to clean, check and fuel each car in between journalists. If there was a gap between them, I would take some of the more interesting ones home. These included the V10 Dodge Ram and the Dodge Viper, all of which was good fun. I remember taking my kids out one at a time in the Viper, thinking they might be excited, but they both fell asleep.....even at way, way over the speed limit (on a private test track M'lud).

The Ram just fitted in my garage with 1 cm to spare in the height. Now that was a beast!

With the addition of the Chrysler and Jeep Franchise, we totally outgrew our Charing Cross location, so it was decided to move the operation to Colston Road in Bishopbriggs, a large operation under the name of Weir Nissan, another one of John Martins aliases.

We were given the workshop at the arse end of the premises, prone to flooding when it rained. What has this come to, the rot had set in....

In the final months, I was just myself in the workshop, so offered the management a deal if they wanted me to stay on. First thing in the morning, I would deal with customers and get the cars organised for the day. Then I would physically service and repair the cars, culminating in invoicing and seeing customers later in the afternoon.

For this, over and above my salary and company car, we agreed that I would receive 15% of my labour sales as a bonus. This worked well until the end, with me making a very good living, as generally I could sell some 30+ hours per week.

When I gave in my notice to go and work for Douglas Park, they swindled me out of the previous months bonus of approx £1200, and when confronted they said "well you have a bad debt of £1200 from a customer so we're not paying you!" I knew the customer in question, who were always slow payers, and offered to collect the debt, enabling me to get paid. It doesn't work that way they said – so bugger them, I'm well out of that company!
I did make a lot of good friends among the staff, some of whom still keep in touch. The amount of gifts and good wishes I received from them on leaving touched me more than I can say...I still have the card with all the good wishes, and even still have a shirt the gave me, and it still fits! Maybe someday it will come back into fashion......

Before I finish this chapter, I just remembered about Willie Curry, you may remember him from a previous chapter. Now Willie was a great mechanic, but messy...gawd he was messy and his tools and toolbox were shocking. One Sunday, me and Derek Ferrar (aka "Deek" who will feature in another chapter) decided we would come in and paint Willies toolbox. The "Snap-On" red paint was obtained, and we resprayed his box, ready for Monday. Boy was Willie upset, in fact he was *bealin!
I was more annoyed that when I took my trousers off afterwards, the bottoms of my trousers were also "Snap-On" red from the overspray!!

* "bealin" is a Scots word meaning angry, outraged, or rather miffed.

Also just remembered something else, the time I got my picture in the Evening Times newspaper. I was out testing a Rolls-Royce, and it ran out of petrol. I was under the bonnet checking, and some bugger took my picture and sent it in to the paper. Fame at last!

While at North Street, this lad came into the showroom claiming to fix dents without having to do any paintwork. Never heard of this, so I was about to chase him, when he offered to fix three tiny dents in a Jaguar door, free, and if we were happy, would we use him going forwards? He did, we did, and I've used Willie Nicol since then as he, I reckon was the original, and still the best in the business.

Anyway, I digress again...

Chapter Seven - The Douglas Park years
(January 12th 1999 until 4th of February 2019)

I had my interview with Ian McKay, the managing director at that time, in the head office on Bothwell Road. Later on, as the group grew, a new purpose built BMW dealership and head office was built just along the road, the old head office is now The Spice Indian Restaurant….

I started work with, as it was then, "Park's Rolls-Royce and Bentley" on Monday, 12th of January 1999. (coincidentally Gordon Clifton's birthday, more of Gordon later)

I went in the previous Saturday to collect my company car, and as soon as I went into the workshop, I wanted to turn on my heels and walk back out! The place was a tip, a midden, a dump, a horror story, a coup, a tip, whatever best describes it….in fact all of them! They (now we) were Chrysler and Jeep dealers as well, and there was a Jeep diesel engine stripped lying in a wheel barrow, leaking oil all over the already filthy workshop floor. Things would be changing!

Monday came, and I was introduced to Gordon Clifton, who at that time was, I would say, the group assistant aftersales manager, the group being nowhere near the size it is currently. Gordon was a bit like Marmite, you either liked him or didn't…...the jury was out with me on that one, but as the years went by, Gordon was my mentor, and we became very good friends.

Later on, with the group growing in size, new blood was brought into head office, some good, some not so good, and it was decided that Gordon was to be charge of the Skoda dealership aftersales department. Gordon should have retired at 65 several years ago, but Gordon being Gordon, carried on working. When I started writing this, Gordon was aftersales manager at Park's Maserati in Almada street. When Gordon turned 65, not a word, gift or anything was forthcoming from head office, I thought that was bang out of order, so I went into the Argyll Arcade in Glasgow and bought Gordon a gold pocket watch as a symbol of my appreciation for all the times he had helped me.

I keep in touch with Gordon, who has since been "encouraged" to retire on 31st of August 2020. He left, with no words of thanks, and had to get a lift home – shoddy treatment for someone who has been a loyal and devoted member of Park's of Hamilton for a great many years.

I had brought my customer database with me from Murray Motors. My days were spent inputting all the details into one of those new fangled computers, as until we were really up and running, there wasn't much in the way of work other than the Chrysler side of things. There was in place a service manager for the Jeep side, but he was soon to leave, and I was in charge of the whole shooting match!

I met the staff, who were a good bunch, including the head mechanic, Storm Dominic O'Reilly Combrink (yes, really), originally from South Africa. He was a great mechanic, but manky! It was him that left the Jeep engine in the wheelbarrow I previously mentioned. Things would definitely be changing!

I had to utilise the existing staff until business built up enough to warrant additional staff, the first job we had in was to replace a broken front road spring on a Bentley Turbo R. The car belonged to Malcolm Clark, who to this day is a good friend, and we regularly keep in touch. With my guidance, Storm replaced the broken spring no problem. Park's Rolls-Royce and Bentley were now up and running!

I must mention two of the directors, who always went everywhere together, usually dressed in long black coats. They were Ian Miller and Robert Wyper, who were known as the two windys, Windy Miller and Windy Wyper. Get it?

I organised another service week or clinic, where customers cars were checked by our guys, along with two technicians from the factory at Crewe. The Crewe guys were put up in the Avonbridge Hotel, just along the road from us, at our cost. I got a phone call from our financial director shortly after the service week was over, refusing to pay for the two pints of beer each evening while they were there.
Now, being fairly new to the company, I wasn't really aware of how important this guy was, so gave him both barrels! One of the factory engineers had shortly before, organised a new engine out of warranty for one of our customers, and head office were quibbling over such a paltry amount….needless to say, the bill was paid. Probably didn't do me any favours, but what the hell!

A few years later, the decision was made to get rid of Chrysler and Jeep, and in its place, put Skoda. Now at that time, Skoda was, and still is to a certain extent, a subject of ridicule. Little do those sceptics know that Skoda is a very good car. My company cars were previously Jeeps, whether it be a Cherokee or a grand Cherokee, but with our demise of Chrysler, I chose a Skoda Octavia VRS, which was duly *"chipped" to produce 225 brake horsepower. My son, when I took it home for the first time, was slightly embarrassed to put it mildly – "dad's got a Skoda!" His opinion soon changed when I took him out in it! I had that car up at 160mph (on a private airfield m'lud)....I loved it.

*Chipped, for those of you less mechanically minded, involves re-mapping the engine management system to alter the power characteristics, as usually the factory setting is a compromise between fuel consumption, emissions, and longevity. Doing so does however invalidate the engines warranty if discovered.

We had a few issues with the site in Townhead street, Bentley weren't best pleased with sharing with Skoda, nor was I, but we all knew this was only temporary, as a new solus Bentley dealership was due to get built. It would be only Bentley, as the split from Rolls-Royce in 2002, meant that we only catered for Crewe built Rolls-Royce.

We had a rather expensive double sided Bentley sign bolted to the side of the building, protruding above the pavement. It didn't last very long before a TNT delivery truck parked with two wheels up on the kerb and knocked it from its mountings, although still suspended there. A hi-ab crane had to be utilised to remove the dangerous sign. It was duly repaired and remounted, until another TNT driver did the same, although this time much worse, as the truck was jammed against the fallen sign and could not be moved.
Hi-ab once again, and the sign was repaired, but never re-hung as a move to our new premises was not that far away. The sign was put into storage, and lay in the storage facility in the new place for many years. We could not mount it, as the cladding on the walls were never designed to take the weight. Latterly, it became a nuisance and we needed the space it took up. It was to be scrapped, but not before I had stripped it and removed the two Bentley "Wings"!
Both adorned my garage, until I gave one to my best pal.

We had a few interesting customers, a lot of taxi drivers, who in general were decent people. Skodas were very popular with the taxi boys, due to the unlimited mileage warranty for 3 years at that time.

Picture the scene, there was one time that a rather large sweaty taxi driver was sitting in the customer lounge, slugging Irn Bru, and counting his change, alongside a Bentley customer who had just spent upwards of £150,000 on a new car.....now I'm not a snob, (well, maybe a wee bit) but this was wrong on so many levels.

This same taxi driver, about two minutes after collecting his Skoda, came back in in a fit of rage, claiming that someone in the workshop had taken a drink out the half empty bottle of coke he had left in the car! Really?

Russell Forsyth (remember him?) was general sales manager at the time, and had been a crucial part in obtaining the Rolls-Royce and Bentley franchise for Douglas Park. Russell had been pivotal in building up an order bank for the new Continental GT, but I reckon lost focus due to some health problems with his daughter, which I won't go into, but let it be said, I attended two disciplinary hearings where head office pulled no punches, in fact I was told to be quiet when I tried to speak up for him, as I was only present as a witness to the proceedings.

One of the issues was that Russell had delivered a Bentley Arnage extended wheelbase car to a certain client, and had accepted a cheque for payment of over £150,000! A strict no-no! He should have waited on cleared funds, but a check from this customer was as good as the Bank of England. No matter, he didn't follow company procedure.

The directors did not find it amusing when we were being ushered into the boardroom for the second hearing, I said "usual seats then?"

It was the beginning of the end for Russell, and he was told to clear his desk. Sad, after all the hard work he had put in. I later heard he had taken them to an industrial tribunal, but was settled out of court I believe. This was never confirmed.

A new general manager was appointed, a chap called Gavin Paterson (more of him later). I didn't take to him very much, as he interfered a lot in my aftersales operation, one of these "know all know fuck alls".

Russell had branched out on his own, trading cars from his house. I had sold him a new set of Bentley alloy wheels at several thousand pounds, and gave him 10% trade discount.

I thought no more of it until a week or two later, I was on holiday when I got a phone call from Gavin, trying to tear me to ribbons for selling Russell wheels, but not only that, giving him discount! I told him to fuck off and hung up on him!

When I returned from holiday, I found a gift wrapped package on my desk. It was a magicians box of tricks (Gavin knew I was an amateur magician). Gavin came in and apologised for his attitude on the phone. After the call, he had gone to see Douglas Park to tell him what I'd done, at which point Douglas gave him a bollocking, saying that I was quite right, and we were happy to take Russells money! After that, Gavin and I had a more tolerant working relationship.

Gavin, however, was very adept at upsetting customers. A couple in particular stand out. The first being my friend Ian Weir, who saw a Porsche 911 in our showroom, and thought his wife Tracy would like it, as she was in the market for a new car. Ian said to Gavin he'd be back in half an hour with his wife.

They came back half an hour later and were looking at the Porsche. Gavin shouted across the showroom "don't bother looking, I've just sold it!"

Gavin was very lucky he didn't have a sore face that day, but Ian took all his custom to Bentley Edinburgh, only returning once Gavin had left.

Another time was when we had a pre-production Continental GT in the showroom to give customers a physical idea of the car, as no one had seen it in the flesh. My friend and loyal customer Gerry Begley phoned in and spoke to Gavin, asking how long the GT would be there, as Gerry wanted to bring his wife Irene through to see it. "The cars going away at seven o'clock" said Gavin, "so by all means come and see it."

It was just after six o'clock and there was no customers in the showroom, so Gavin ordered the GT to be loaded onto the covered transporter earlier than planned. About six thirty, Gerry and Irene came in to find the car hidden away in the lorry. Not happy, Gerry confronted Gavin, who just said, "you can have a look inside the transporter if you want!" Gerry was very disappointed and vowed never to return.

The next day, I had very strong words with Gavin, and insisted he do something to rectify his shoddy treatment of our customers. We agreed to offer Gerry the use of our demonstration Arnage T, and organised a factory VIP visit for Gerry and his guests. Gerry was delighted, and often speaks of both the car, and the visit. In fact he went on to purchase an Arnage of his own.

Gavin rested on his laurels as the new Continental GT became available, in fact he took the credit for the huge upturn in sales, but he was just in the right place at the right time. We became one of the most profitable dealers in the whole group.

These new Bentleys were very much in demand, and fetching up to £25,000 over list price. Allegedly there were a few "ghost" orders placed, so I heard, adding to the already decent profit margin. This of course never happened with us!

We had acquired the Bentley Le Mans race car for a showroom event, and I bet Gavin a tenner he couldn't get into it. He very nearly did, but struggled to get out, Gavin being quite a chubby guy, and the car cockpit was designed for small lightweight racing drivers.

My Grandson Dylan in the cockpit
(He was considerably smaller than Gavin!)

I had a good team under me, and I thought both as a reward, and to spark a bit more enthusiasm, I decided to organise a factory visit for the apprentices. My company car at the time was a seven seat Land Rover Discovery, so was ideal for the trip.

The visit went particularly well at the factory, so I thought as a wee treat we would call in to Blackpool on the way home for fish and chips. We also went to a pub I knew, and had a few games of pool. All in all a very successful day, but back to work in the morning.

Factory Visit, Left to Right:
Russell Smith Apprentice Technician
Craig Pryde Parts Department Apprentice
Jonny Stevenson Apprentice Technician
Lois – Factory Receptionist
Myself
Cumfy John Apprentice Technician
(I'm not fat, I'm comfortable - his words)

I had sported a large moustache for a good many years, and thought it time for a change. Why not arrange something that would maybe benefit charity? I made up some posters, and spread them around the dealership, asking for donations to the cash for kids charity if I shaved the 'tache off. Customers weren't shy in putting their hands in their pockets and purses under my encouragement.

The day came, and I had arranged Tracy Weir, my good friends wife to come in and do the deed. Tracy was a hairdresser in a previous life, so seemed the ideal choice, and always up for a laugh. I sat on a stool in the middle of the showroom while Tracy did the necessary, keeping the moustache in a little tin that used to house Bentley mint sweets!

I raised £368 for cash for kids which was good. I've lost the tin however, It may turn up at some point. It was all a laugh, the trade used to be like that…..

We moved to the new custom built solus premises in Bothwell Road on the 9th of May 2005 in time (almost) for the launch of the new Continental Flying Spur. I say almost, as the showroom floor hadn't been tiled yet, but no one at the launch seemed to mind, being more excited about the new car.

Our name also changed from "Park's Rolls-Royce and Bentley" to "Bentley Glasgow" in line with what Bentley were trying to achieve with dealers being named after the nearest city. Just as well we weren't near Ecclefechan, Auchenshuggle or Auchtermuchty! Some dealers, Jack Barclay in London for one, refused to change their name. They got away with it as they were the oldest and biggest dealer in the world.

We had a used car display at the front of the building, and often we would find golf balls lying around the cars. As there was student accommodation across the road from us, we suspected them of throwing the golf balls at the car display. I wasn't until some time later, I was around the back, having a well earned fag break, and a crow flew overhead with a golf ball in its beak. It dropped the ball, which bounced, over a new car, narrowly missing it. The ball came to rest under the fence, and was chased by the crow, but I got there first. Turns out the golf balls were nicked from the golf driving range down the road. Poor students getting the blame, when it was the crows all along. They must have thought the balls were eggs or something.

Another time, a few years ago during a particularly bad snowfall, traffic came to a standstill in Bothwell Road, so I waited a few hours to see if it cleared. No chance, cars abandoned everywhere, so no chance of getting home. There wasn't a single hotel room available anywhere in Hamilton, so it was decided myself, a van driver, and our parts guy, would need to spend the night in the dealership.

First though, food. We walked down to the Spice Indian restaurant, which was mobbed by people with the same idea as us. There was very little staff on, as the owner never expected to be busy. Anyway, three hours later we were fed, and walked back to the dealership, passing our sister BMW company, where most of the staff were also staying.

Back in the showroom, we settled down in the customer lounge, and I cracked open a bottle of malt Whisky a customer had given me earlier. Around midnight, we heard a commotion outside, and saw the aforesaid mentioned students having a snowball fight on the roundabout.

Next thing we new, they had all stripped off bollock naked, and continued with the snowball fight. That didn't last long however, it was bloody freezing. We settled down, each of us finding a warm place to sleep, I took a Bentley car cover and that was to be my duvet for the night. Back to work next morning, by which time, a lot of the traffic had cleared. We had a great laugh, a lot of banter, and whisky – great combination.

Gavin's reign was to be fairly short lived, more of Gavin later on unfortunately. The sales team had won an eight grand Bentley Breitling watch for some performance or other. Gavin, as the "leader" claimed it for himself. In a subsequent conversation with Douglas Park in head office, Gavin showed Douglas the watch. "That's fine, just leave it on my desk when you go out" said Douglas - Gavin was not a happy chappie.

He "left" in April 2006 and started up his own business, this lasted just 19 months, then he headed for Bentley Edinburgh, then the middle East. Enough for the moment about Gavin, but our paths were due to cross again.

A new general manager, Alastair Paterson was appointed. Big Al was a really nice guy, came from a Porsche background, and was just what we needed. He was flamboyant, long blond hair and a beard. The customers loved him, and he brought a few Porsche customers with him, one of whom was John Reid, lead singer of the Nightcrawlers, who I became friends with and still keep in touch, although at time of writing, he is in Los Angeles, living a jet set lifestyle, having re-released and re edited his anthem Push the Feeling On, a major hit for him in 2003. John is a prolific writer, having written songs for many big show biz names.

I remember one time I was on the phone to a customer who I hadn't seen for a while. I enquired what line of business he was in nowadays, and he replied selling herbal Viagra on line, and making a fortune. Not that I needed it, but he sent me a complimentary couple of bottles, one male and one female. I mentioned this to Al, and he asked for some pills one Friday evening at close of business.

I obliged, as his "friend" was waiting in the customer lounge for him. I was half way home, and my mobile rang. This was Pedro, one of our sales guys, and he could hardly speak for laughing. Apparently Al had swallowed half a dozen of the pills, and his face and ears turned bright red. He was also downing litres of water as he was burning up. In the words of Pedro, his ears looked like raw steaks!

Al was a bit of a drama queen, and would regularly have hissy fits if things weren't going his way. Another time I went into his office, and he was banging his mobile phone against the desk. I tried to calm him down, but he said "it's my phone and I'll do what I like", to which I replied, aye, but its not your desk, which by this time was badly marked.

The ladies loved Big Al...

One morning, I went round the back to open up, and the rear workshop door was damaged and the handle broken off. I thought we had a burglary. Not so, it was big Al the previous night. Turns out, he had been waiting on a transporter delivery around 10:00pm, and when the transporter arrived, Al went out to meet it. It was raining, he had no jacket on, left his phone and keys in his office, and totally forgot the showroom doors automatically locked on exiting! He tried to force the back door, breaking the handle in the process, and unable to get in, walked to our petrol kiosk, where he phoned Neil McCallum, who came to his rescue.

Yet another time, in a fit of rage, in the pouring rain, he reversed his Range Rover by accident, into a customers Bentley parked around the back of the dealership. Everyone was at fault except Alistair. I had to call the customer the next day to explain what had happened, the customer was more annoyed that Al hadn't phoned him personally, leaving the dirty work to me. The customer jumped into one of his other cars, and met me at our bodyshop to confirm the damage to be as I had described, which it was. For once, the bodyshop made a great job of the repair, so much so that when the customer damaged his Range Rover, he gave it to the bodyshop to fix. Unfortunately they mucked him about and he phoned me to get it sorted.
Al, as I said, was a good guy, but never really a general manager, I remember him out in the car park filling in a pothole, in full view of head office. They were not happy. Al left not long after that.

Next in the GM role was Lee Martis, brought in from or neighbouring Douglas Park BMW. I knew Lee from BMW, and I also knew his father who was a car dealer, and had at one time or another owned several Bentleys.

We had the franchise for Maserati for a while, until it was moved to Almada Street, and McLaren was taken on, temporarily at first in Almada Street until the new purpose built facility was finished, right next to Bentley. I was also given charge of the aftersales side of McLaren too, which I thought was quite exciting. I had some good trips with McLaren, their "Welcome to McLaren" trip was amazing, learning all the history of the marque, followed by driving the cars around the racetrack, followed by a visit to the McLaren factory. Awesome does not describe it enough.

Lee was given the task of GM for not only Bentley, but McLaren and Maserati also….hmm, big job, maybe too much for one guy, but time would tell…

My being in charge of the aftersales departments for both Bentley and McLaren, although fun and a challenge in the beginning, soon turned into the opposite. More of that later.

The new purpose built McLaren facility eventually was completed, and it was the day of the official launch. There was an issue with one of the built in televisions, which had to be fixed before the launch evening. Our "in house" electricians were called in. Due to some clever planning, one of the booths had to be partially dismantled to allow access to the TV. Disaster struck, when the roof of the booth fell down, damaging the desk, two chairs, and one of the segments of the roller shutter cupboard door. Now, to put you in the picture, the McLaren showroom was state of the art, and had electronic roller shutters in each booth, which had anything from paint colour samples to keyrings. Panic set in, as a replacement shutter would be several weeks away, and involved major stripping to replace.

Now, one of my friends, Stuart Elrick, and very talented cosmetic repairer had his place just along the road. Stuart (AKA "Stu the Painter") was frowned upon by head office, as he was deemed to be taking work away from our own bodyshop. I gave Stu a call, and he dropped everything and came right over.

The guy is a miracle worker, and repaired the roller shutter, the desk, and the chairs which was undetectable, and indeed are still in use today. This did him no harm, and was greatly appreciated by head office for digging us out of a hole.

The opening went very well, helped by the David Coulthard formula one car we had on loan from McLaren.

We went on to achieve a few awards, namely European dealer of the year in 2015, then onwards to Global retailer of the year in 2015, then European dealer of the year in 2016 and then Global retailer the same year, then European dealer of the year in 2018. Missed out on 2017 which was won by McLaren Ascot.

These awards were benchmarked using an extensive assessment process, and rated in key areas including sales, customer service, aftersales and marketing.

Above, Just some of the McLaren Glasgow team with the 2015 award.
Left to right:
Scott McGee - Aftersales Advisor, Myself - Aftersales Manager,
Craig Handley – Product Genius, Colin Benbow – Master Technician,
Anita Hughes – Showroom Host, Lee Martis – General Manager.

Photo courtesy of Park's of Hamilton website

Bentley in their infinite wisdom, decided that all the dealerships should undergo a facelift and along with a new corporate identity I reckoned it cost us in the region of £400,000!

The showroom floor was to be re-tiled, so the new tiles were laid on top of the previous ones – worked okay, but not a huge difference in the colour. All the furniture had to go and a skip was put out the back to dispose of it. The beautiful leather suite from the customer lounge went up to head office, but the rest was for the bin! Aye right! It started with Lee our GM asking Ross Park if he could take his office chair, as it had many years of his bum print embossed on it. Ross agreed which opened the flood gates for me. I got 3 chairs, a display cabinet, the lounge table, some framed photographs, and seven pictures and frames. Lee remarked I had so much stuff, I rolled out my bed in the morning and would think I was at work!

The table turned out to be a bit of a disaster. Three of us carried it into our big lounge and thought no more. The following morning I went into the lounge and found the glass table top had shattered into every corner of the room. We were hoovering up broken glass for months! Reckon it may have been stressed during the transportation, who knows. I'm proud of the table now though, I'd moved it into my newly redecorated man-cave, but the green colour didn't go with the grey/blue décor. I ain't going to get rid, it was a very expensive and well made table, I'd saved it once, I'll do it again. Ebay to the rescue...I ordered several metres of carbon fibre vinyl wrapping, and covered the full table. Again, from Ebay, I ordered a 10mm thick, metre square toughened glass table protector. I have to say I'm delighted with the result.

Lee was to relinquish Bentley, and concentrate on McLaren and Maserati, so a new GM for Bentley was needed. This was a chap called Gavin Stephenson. Gavin was from an Audi background and a nice guy. Myself and my wife went to London with Gavin and his then Fianceé Nikki, now his wife, to a Bentley Grand ball in 2018.

Gavin was later to move onto new horizons, working for the Rolls-Royce dealership in Edinburgh.
He took Derek, our best salesman with him later on. As it turned out, wasn't the best move, as Rolls-Royce Edinburgh would go into administration. After a stint with Audi, he is now back with Park's, in the role of sales manager with Maserati.

Back to Gavin Paterson again, Ross Park phoned me one evening to say that Gavin Paterson would be starting the following morning as General Manager, would I have an issue with that? Ross thought it better I heard it from him rather than get it sprung on me in the morning. Not a problem, I'll work with anyone.

According to Gavin, he had previously been offered the job at Bentley but declined it. At that point he was general manager at Douglas Park BMW in Stirling, and was doing well there. Allegedly, he was given his marching orders, as head office had already appointed a replacement for him. Gavin then accepted the Bentley position, and asked why as he had previously declined it, well he replied he didn't know he would be out of a job if he didn't take it!

There is no doubt more to this, but guess we'll never find out.

Gavin and I, although having a few disagreements, for the most part got on okay.

One day one of the drivers came up to me, saying Gavin had told them not to wash service cars forthwith, as they were there to drive only. I went ballistic, storming into Gavins office, shutting the door behind me. Suffice to say, the drivers still carried out service washes. The alternative was supposed to be to get the valet department to do service washes, this was tried before and was totally impractical, as the sales department had the valeters going full out, and it wouldn't be taken kindly to take them off sales work to clean a customers car.

Gavin was the subject of a "Forbidden Scotland" sting on video, and has since been charged with offences relating to sending inappropriate messages and explicit images to a 13 year old girl, and was granted bail. In the press, a Park's spokesman said "this person no longer works for us" At the time of writing, Gavin has not been seen or heard of…...you think you know somebody!

In a previous chapter at Murray Motor Company, I mentioned Bentley Area Service Managers (ASM).

When Park's took the Franchise on, our ASM was a great chap called James Long. James was Irish, and a bit of a racing driver. He would often bring me parts of his racing car which got damaged, and I would get them fixed at our bodyshop. Ron Chunn was next in line, another good guy who knew the best "titty bars" when we went on various Elite club jaunts.

Our next ASM was a chap called Gavin Hewson, he was a good guy, still a friend on Facebook. Next was a guy, lets just call him "Bob". No one could ever get hold of him, and one day, he was taking his boss Steve Graham around the dealer network, and got lost trying to find our dealership coming from Bentley Edinburgh! I must mention that he had been at us several times before.

We, and the dealer network decided on the nickname of "the Bentley hide and seek champion".

One of the other ASMs at the time, lets call him Jon, had, while on holiday, allegedly dived into a swimming pool that only had 2 inches of water...he broke his neck, nasty, but still alive and was off work for months.

Now, the reason I mentioned him, was around this time, you may remember, Malaysian Aircraft flight 370 went missing and was never found. Someone came up with the story that it was okay, because it was Rob that was piloting, and Jon was the co-pilot, so although the plane got lost, it just landed in 2 inches of water! I have my thoughts on who came up with that one – Neil?

Next on the ASM list, was my good friend Karl Shirley, who I keep in touch with, play golf and have a bite to eat a few times a year, along with John (Ketchup) Cherry (ex Bentley Edinburgh) and Terry Lee, retired Bentley factory parts manager.

Karl was seconded to set up and run the new CW1 house, Bentleys flagship showroom in Crewe, next to the factory, so our next lad was Jonathan Morris, who I still keep in touch with. On my retirement, Jonathan took me out for dinner, and presented me with a valuable Bentley fountain pen.

Jonathan is still currently ASM, although his role is changing to a more aftersales business manager, concerned more with profitability...

Chapter Eight - My Marketing Strategies...

I always enjoyed a challenge when it came to selling accessories. It's amazing, particularly with our marques, customers are always looking for a wee individual touch to make their car just a touch different.

I really started taking it seriously back in the early nineties, when a customer enquired about fitting Bentley twin headlamps to their Rolls-Royce Spirit. I priced it up, each part, nuts, bolts and screws, and ended up fitting the conversion. The factory were not very happy with me, as this modification was frowned upon. A while later, the factory brought out a full kit of everything needed, which I sold dozens of. I also took this opportunity to market early Mulsanne owners too.

Moving on to when the Arnage Red Label was introduced. I saw a gap in the market for upgrading (in looks only) a customers Arnage Green Label. This consisted of wheels, tyres, front, rear, and side repeater lamps with white lenses, and to finish off, larger rear exhaust trims. I did so many of them that we ran out of room to store the old wheels, so put them out the back of the workshop. One day, one of our neighbours reported some men stealing the wheels, and loading them into a van. That's fine, saves me getting rid of them, as the going rate was only £3 per wheel scrap value.

I was offered a set a couple of weeks later, one of my customers had bought them. You should have seen his face drop when I told him what they were worth. I said he could have had a set for nothing!

With some customers, (I had to choose wisely), if their Arnage Green Label was in for servicing, I would have a set of Red Label Wheels and tyres fitted just before the car was brought round for collection. More often than not, the wheels were bought and stayed on the car. Usually accompanied by a few light hearted comments, generally around me being a cheeky bastard! I don't think I ever had to remove a set, as the difference to the car was quite dramatic.

The Silver Seraph had chrome inserts to the headlamps, which proved to be a popular modification to the Arnage. It was not inexpensive, at over £1500 for the two new lamps, and we did a good few of them.

Many years ago, Bentley had produced a towelling robe, in British Racing Green, with the Bentley logo. I bought one (at a discount of course), and still have it to this day. As Bentley tend to do with these things, once stock was exhausted, that was it – no more.

I once got asked if they still did them, which set me thinking. I sourced a company who could embroider the Bentley Wings Logo along with Bentley Glasgow wording, and they sourced some very good quality robes, and applied the Logo. Three colours were available, white, Black and Magnolia. They sold like hotcakes, in fact Douglas Park bought some (at less discount that I got!)

If you cast your mind back to when I was in Marbella and Bentley gave each of us a Bentley apron, which gave me an idea. Using the same company as before, I had Bentley Glasgow ones produced. They sold at about fifteen quid, and again, they sold like hotcakes, leading up to Christmas.

A customer remarked "what's next? Bentley Glasgow underwear?" Yup, that was next, and black or white boxer shorts were commissioned. At again, fifteen quid, they sold well, after all, what you get the man who has everything?

One of the big wigs, Chris Kelly at Bentley was leaving in March 2011, and I had a pair framed, and I presented it to him at his leaving do...oops, sorry, dealer conference!

Myself and Chris Kelly with the framed
boxer shorts...

Bentley introduced a Mulliner styling kit, but the sales department wouldn't let us fit a kit to their demonstrator, so, copying an idea from Neil Sawyers at Harwoods, I put a kit on the showroom wall.

Bentley also brought out vented front wings, so I had two painted in red and white, and mounted to a stand I found lying around.......

Wall mounted styling kit (cheers Neil)

Vented wing stand

I had Bentayga owner who complained his heated steering wheel was getting too hot. You wouldn't get away with offering a pair of oven gloves to a lot of people, but I knew he had a sense of humour and would find it amusing. I ordered a new steering wheel, but also commissioned Bentley Glasgow oven gloves, which I duly gifted to him. He sent me a photograph with the oven gloves taking pride of place in his kitchen. I ordered a few dozen and put them up for sale, again did very well at twelve quid.

Wasn't quite sure if this should go in the chapter on Jollies, but here ye go…..

Bentley introduced a scheme called Bentley Rewards, basically the more accessories you personally sold, the more points you would get…what do points make? PRIZES! Only a few points for small items, but got really lucrative if you sold things like a set of alloy wheels. That was my forte, and some of the prizes I got were an upmarket toaster and kettle, an Amazon smart speaker, but one of the best things was that you could exchange points for gift cards, that could be used to purchase things, just as you would with a debit card.

Now, we had a young lad in the parts department, and as an incentive, I registered him on the rewards scheme and explained the rules. This, unfortunately was to cost him his job, as firstly, he deliberately claimed points for everything that was bought instead of what he had sold, and secondly, used the points to get cash cards, which he used our card machine to turn it into cash. I had to call Bentley and explain, and he was blocked from any further points. Head office was involved, and he lost his job. The other downside was that nobody else could claim points on anything he had claimed. Probably should have reclaimed the money, but he had already spent it.

Chapter Nine - The "Jollies"

I have had many memorable trips around the world, and indeed the UK, courtesy of, Bentley and McLaren. I also had a few with Aston Martin, Lotus, and Chrysler Jeep, which were a good few years ago.

When we first got the Jeep franchise with Murray Motors, Gary Bagley (my boss) thought it would be a good idea to get some off road training under our belts! As Jeep weren't at the stage of training yet, and the John Marting group having the Vauxhall franchise, Gary told Vauxhall we were two new salesmen, and enrolled us of an off road training course down in the borders….looking forward to that!

We arrived at the training venue first thing in the morning, and were introduced to our transport for the day, a 4 wheel drive Vauxhall Frontera, not quite a Jeep, but still a very capable vehicle. Along with us, there were a family of four (Maw, Paw and the weans) who had just bought a new top of the range Mitsubishi Shogun, and had booked some training in their own vehicle, bad move I'm thinking. Anyway, the morning was pretty tame, driving through fields, over see-saws, and generally a bit of mud. The instructor then took us for lunch in a local pub, at which point the father of the family spilt a full pint of beer right down the front of his trousers…. A portent of things to come I fear!

The lunch finished, we headed for the real stuff, through the forestry commission land. We had to drive down a tree lined route, the trees being just under a cars width apart! This was ok in our Frontera, as it already had been through the wars with any Tom, Dick or Harry at the wheel, not to mention Garry and yours truly, but I felt sorry for our friend in the Shogun, which was even wider than the Frontera, and did suffer badly, it's gleaming new paintwork reduced to a scratched mess!

A few miles later, I saw no sign of Mr Shogun behind us, so we backtracked to see where he had gotten to. We came across him, at a standstill, with a rather large tree branch totally jammed underneath!

A bit of brute force and ignorance soon removed it, and we were back under way. I bet he wished he had paid the extra bucks to use one of the centres vehicles instead of his own.

Anyway, that was the first of many off-road courses I attended, subsequent ones however, were under the Jeep and Bentley banners, and not as Vauxhall salesmen!

One of the more memorable courses were at an off road centre near Stirling, myself, Brian Baldesarra and Alan Potts attended and had a great laugh honing our off road skills.

*Brian, Alan and myself....
A Jeep day and I had my
Aston Martin jacket on!*

All these courses were to benefit me when some years later I had my own Landrover Defender, and had a lot of fun off-roading that.

*My Defender...
Registration
number
CUR55E*

Around 1996, Lotus day at Knockhill with Murray Motor Company

This was a fantastic day, never seen so many Lotuses (or should it be "Lotii?" in one place. A full days entertainment was on offer, including clay pigeon shooting, JCB driving, archery, off road driving, and the bit I enjoyed the most – driving a Lotus Esprit V8 around several laps of Knockhill racing circuit. Russell managed to prang one into the gravel…
The day culminated an a display of all the Lotuses on the racetrack. Knockhill is owned by Derek Butcher, who had a Bentley, and regularly gave me VIP passes to the Knockhill events. I still keep in touch with Derek, one of the good guys.
For those that don't know, Lotus stands for…

"Lots Of Trouble, Usually Serious!"

Much as Fiat stands for

"Fix It Again Tony!"

December 2005, UK dealer conference in Berlin

We flew to Berlin on the 1st December 2005, and stayed at the "Jolly Hotel Vivaldi", which was quite handy for the conference in the head office of Volkswagen. On a tour of the facility, I got my first glimpse of a Bugatti Veyron….
While we were at the conference, our partners had a tour of Berlin, including the famous "Check Point Charlie". I'd probably rather have done that than the conference!
We dined at a beautiful restaurant next to the Brandenburg Gate, just along from the Adlon hotel where Michael Jackson dangled his son over the balcony of the presidential suite! Berlin is a stunning city, but I've never been so cold in my life, well it was the middle of winter, and I had only brought a light jacket!
The Christmas market was awesome, better than any I've ever been to, I did indulge in some Gluhwein and a metre long hot dog!
This was my first Bentley conference, a taste of things to come over the next years.

Bentley Motors ran an "Elite Club" incentive, based on several performance criteria, such as parts performance against target, retail hours sold, customer satisfaction etc. etc. These criteria changed from year to year, making it harder to achieve. It has been known for parts and aftersales managers to over purchase parts at year end just to make the trip. These trips were awesome, no expense spared. I had missed the first trip, which was to Greece, as we were still in the old dealership at Townhead Street, which was only a temporary facility until the new solus dealership was ready in 2005. This temporary site did not have the corporate image or the facility to reach full performance potential, hence no Elite Club for me!

There were several stories about the Greek trip, one being that all those that attended had a little too much drink at the airport and on the plane there, only to be met with a fleet of Volkswagen Touregs, which all the guys were to drive off road. Needless to say, there was not one vehicle that didn't sustain some form of damage! The dealer that lent out the cars couldn't have been best pleased to put it mildly!

In 2005, we had moved to the new dealership in Bothwell Road in Hamilton, and with a healthy performance in 2005, allowed a delegate (me) to go on the trip in April 2006, which was to Tenerife. I had taken it upon myself to nominate me to go, and Bentley sent on the flight tickets. Now, head office open all mail into any of the dealerships, so a few eyebrows were raised when these tickets arrived with my name on them. Next thing I knew, I had a visit from the dealer principal from head office, tearing me to bits for accepting the trip without consulting them. Fortunately, there was a desk between us, otherwise a certain person would have had a sore face for speaking to me like he did!

Anyway, after the group aftersales manager came down and explained to me in a more civilised manner, the reasons behind their stance, I could see where they were coming from. It seems that certain sales managers purchased additional cars just to meet year end targets, enabling them to fraudulently go on the trips other franchises offered as incentives.

There was a big difference in buying a few extra parts to meet target, than to buying a few extra vehicles!

I was allowed to go on the trip, but next time I had to be sure to get head offices approval before accepting anything.

These trips were pretty full on, usually flying out on the Thursday or Friday, and returning on the Monday or Tuesday of the following week.

April 2006 Elite Club - Tenerife

We arrived at the five star Gran Hotel Bahia del Duque resort, which I've got to say was one of the best hotels I've ever stayed in.

Robbie Williams (who?) had stayed there the week before, shame it wasn't the same week, we could have had a wee sing song!
Speaking of sing songs, on the first night, we went into the Playa De Las Americas, suitably led by Ron Chunn, one of our hosts from Bentley, who had researched the best lap dancing clubs (or titty bars). While in one of those establishments (I had to go, they all made me), we had a whip round (not literally) and bought our host a private lap dance, behind screens in the main area. One of our party who shall remain nameless (sorry Sean) decided to film the proceedings by reaching his camera phone over the screen. The young lady who was performing the dance grabbed the phone and launched it across the bar! How we laughed.....

Anyway, after a night in the pubs and clubs, we headed back to the hotel. I reckon there were over 20 of us, as there were also delegates from dealerships in Europe. When we reached the hotel, there was an orchestral and choral performance taking place in one of the many hotel amphitheatres.

We were admiring the show from a balcony above, (here is where the sing song I mentioned earlier comes in) so we all decided to sing along to their rendition of "O Sole Mio", or as our version went "Just one cornetto".
In any normal hotel, we would have been chucked out, but to give the manager his due, he tactfully approached us and said he had laid on complimentary drinks in a bar in another area of the hotel, and perhaps we would all be happier there…...no need to ask twice!

The hotel charges were extortionate, as one would expect in a five star establishment, fortunately Bentley had everything covered. One exception to this was, on the first day, I had left my sun tan lotion on the hotel bar (us gingers need to be really careful) and it was gone when I went back for it. Thieving buggers! No problem, I'll just buy another in the hotel shop. £39 later for a bottle of Ambre Solaire…I should just have let myself get burnt!

The following day, we had a most memorable trip up the mountains in a fleet of open top Landrovers…..weather was beautiful as you would expect.

Can't quite recall what we did that night, I'm sure someone must have tampered with my diet coke! I do remember at some point, myself and Ricky from Bentley Edinburgh were sitting at a table in the hotel bar, and the barman got fed up with our constantly going up to the bar for another round, he just gave us a bottle of whisky. I seem to remember it evaporated pretty damn quickly in the heat!

Anyway, the following day we all went out in catamarans, looking for whales and dolphins.

I've never been seasick in my life before, but this time I was sitting next to one of the southern dealers, and he just threw up! That set me off, and I did the same...and to this day, I always get seasick, I'm sure its psychological, but as my psychiatrist charges me double because I'm schizophrenic, I'll just live with it.

Myself accepting the award from Ron Chunn, Bentley host and UK area manager, on behalf of the Bentley Glasgow Aftersales team.

The hotel had its own private beach, not that we were interested in sunbathing, but the jet skis looked a much more exciting prospect!

As it was our last afternoon, so Ricky and I paid our money, donned our life jackets and headed out to sea, or so we thought. They had laid out a course of bhoys which we had to adhere to, pretty tame, but that didn't stop us going like f#ck!

We came back pretty sore, but with big grins on our faces!

On the last night, returning from the usual pubs around 2 or 3.00am, it was decided to go swimming in one of the many hotel pools. This later became a tradition for future trips. Now, we didn't go back for our trunks, so we just went in with our underwear (glad I hadn't gone commando on that occasion!).

As you may or may not know, Tenerife is on a volcanic island, subsequently some of the hotel swimming pools were formed around rather sharp volcanic rock. One such rock I decided to climb, lost my balance and fell backwards into a cactus! This resulted in my back being severely scratched, try explaining that when I got home!

So that pretty much brings us to the end of my first Elite Club trip, Ricky and I flew back to Glasgow, had a man cuddle, and said cheerio, until the next time.

A few days after I got back, I got a phone call from my mum telling me dad wasn't well. I rushed home, calling an ambulance on the way. My dad was sitting on the settee, and just died. The paramedics tried to revive him, but unsuccessfully. I was supposed to be attending a Bentley customer dinner that evening, Neil went in my place. My dads last words were "for fucks sake woman, you nearly took my ears off"! My mum had pulled his pullover over his head as he was complaining of being too hot.….end of an era.…

My dad used to give me three rings at 6:30am every morning, and I would give him three rings back.…one of those days just before he died, the three rings turned into four, five, six.…..so I picked up the phone. He told me he was proud of me, I think he knew his time was coming.…

My life was about to change, as I moved in with my disabled mum, to look after her. Anyway, this is about my time in the motor trade, but I just had to mention my dad, still miss him.

At the end of 2006, we had met the requirements to qualify for the Elite Club, but it wasn't revealed where we would be going. It was later announced that it would be in April, and we were off to Malta, something to look forward to.

December 2006 Dealer Conference, Gleneagles.

It Was decided that the Scottish contingent should all hire the Saltire kilt outfits, which we did, myself, John Cherry and Ricky Smith. I'm glad we didn't have to pay for drinks at Gleneagles prices! I had previously met Ricky when we were on the Elite club trip to Tenerife, so I knew that a good few Whiskies would be downed. We walked into the evening "do" resplendent in our kilts, and armed with a wee Dram.

It went on until the wee small hours, and the management had to eject us from the hot tub by the leisure centre at 7.30am… still talked about to this day! Ohh, I meant to say we also had a dealer conference I think.

01/12/2006

From Left to Right: John Cherry and Ricky Smith, from Bentley Edinburgh, and yours truly, armed with some wee Drams

April 2007 Elite Club - Malta

April soon came and we were off….we arrived at the Hilton in St Juliens, another stunning hotel overlooking the marina.

Again, it was going to be a full on few days, starting with the first night, our host had arranged a salsa club, which was different to the usual bars we frequented. Many cocktails were consumed that evening!

Just a few of us with our non-alcoholic drinks… (Aye, Right!)

The following day, we went to Malta airport, where we all went up in light aircraft and had a flight around the island.

This was followed by a tour of the fire station and demonstration of the equipment….we could only get a short demonstration, as they didn't have enough funding for any more, and had to keep the foam in case of a real emergency!

In the evening, we had the award presentation, where each delegate was given a certificate in recognition of their respective dealerships performance. followed by dinner and a few more drinks..

Certificate presentation....
Left to right:
Terry Lee (Bentley Host)
Myself
Ron Chunn (Bentley Host)

The following day, we went to the coast, and were split into teams. Each team was allocated a speedboat with a skipper, and we were to take part in a treasure hunt around the island. Funnily, I didn't get seasick this time, I guess the adrenalin rush had something to do with it!

I must mention Jane, who was one of the English aftersales managers, a rarity for a female then. She was a great sport, one of our tasks was to fill a 6 foot tall tube with seawater, using a measuring jug. The downside was the tube was full of holes, like a flute. Jane, bless her, clad in her bikini, wrapped herself around the tube, and being lovely and curvy, she covered most of the holes! Our team won – no contest!

Left to right:
Ron Chunn (Bentley Host)
Myself
Barry Hopkinson
(Bentley Leicester)

What a great day, all was going well until it was time to return, the sea turned very rough, we were bounced about in the little boat to the point where I was sure my internal organs had become dislodged! We had tell the skipper to slow down a bit, and we found the best position was to stand at the stern (rear, for those of you who have not got a nautical disposition) of the boat, where it was less turbulent. I must say, I was glad to get back on dry land! The next day, it was time to go home, another very successful and enjoyable trip. It was now 2007, and yet again, we qualified for the Elite Club, destination in 2008 was to be Marrakesh, in Morocco – sounds interesting.

December 2007 – Dealer conference.

This was held in a beautiful hotel in the Cotswolds called the Lygon Arms. For the evening we were ferried to the Broadway Tower Castle, where we climbed a spiral staircase up to the banqueting hall, where the meals and entertainment was laid on.

Somebody must have force fed me alcohol, then threw me up on the stage, resplendent in my full Saltire kilt outfit, where I was forced to sing with the band!

A most memorable evening, maybe for the wrong reasons…

May 2008 Elite Club – Marrakesh, Morocco.

Here we are in Marrakesh, in Morocco. Top hotel as usual, and a few days of activities lined up.

One of which was "Donkey polo", where you had to hit a ball with a broom, while sitting on a donkey, being guided by one of your team. A few of us thought this was cruel to the donkeys, but they seemed well cared for, and their owners a least got some money in what was an extremely poor country. The other activities that day included five a side football, wall climbing, camel riding (my camel had three humps, I called him Humphrey), quad biking and assembling a tent.

Our illustrious team

A few of the places we went, we were crowded by young children begging. One of our number made the mistake of throwing his Bentley cap into the crowd of kids, and most others did the same. Unfortunately this caused some of the children to kick lumps out of each other in an attempt to secure a cap. Reminded me a bit of the old scrambles we had at weddings when I was a wee boy, the best man throwing out a handful of coins from the wedding car. Anyway, I digress again.

One of the restaurants had lined up a guard of honour called the Blue Men for us at the entrance. After a great meal and several drinks, time to get the coach back to the hotel. Everyone back on board, then all hell broke loose. The manager and some staff stopped the coach, came on board, and demanded that their stolen property was returned. Turns out, two of the young European guests had not finished their drinks, and boarded the coach carrying the glasses. They soon apologised, returned the glasses and we were free to go.

I believe I may have joined in with the belly dancers, someone must have spiked my drink! Probably those damned Europeans!

Yours truly showing how it should be done!

The Blue Men Guard of Honour

Karl Shirley presenting the obligatory certificate

One of the days, we explored the markets, or Souks to give them their proper title. It had not rained for several months, and guess what? The heavens opened up, the locals were loving it and dancing in the puddles. Us? We huddled together under shelter until it died down a bit. It was warm rain though, slightly warmer than Scottish rain.

Pouring from the heavens...

Abdul, our guide, taught us how to make Moroccan mint tea, and gave us a tour of one of the local villages. Strange to see such poor living conditions, but most had a satellite dish and television. Abdul was to continue his guiding with a broken ankle, having suffered a bad tackle during our five a side football – Mr Karl Shirley was the perpetrator I believe?

The group ready for the off...

November 2008 – Dealer conference, Balmoral Hotel, Edinburgh.

Another "dealer conference" or annual piss-up. This time closer to home. As usual, the Scots amongst us wore our kilts, and historically some of the English ladies would delight in saying "what you got under your kilt then Jock" and proceed to lift your kilt up. This time was going to be different. I had purchased a G-string, with the head of a cock (get your minds out the gutter, it was a male chicken!) and if any of the ladies asked what was under my kilt, I would respond with "do you want to see my cock?"

This was hilarious, particularly if the "cock" was squeezed, it would emit a loud "cock-a-doodle-do". I did my usual magic tricks, but as the evening went on, alcohol took an effect, in as much as I dropped a full pack of cards while shuffling them, but to everyone's astonishment, the card that had been picked fell face upwards, while the rest of the pack fell face down. I decided to finish on a high!

A few of us went down to the hotel cocktail bar, and myself and Jimmy Ellis went to the bar to get the drinks in. We had the barmen eating out the palm of our hand as we asked them to make up several different cocktails for us to sample. We eventually went back to the table with the round, and I remember asking Jimmy if he had paid for the drinks as I hadn't. No was the reply, I guess of the two barmen that served us, each thought the other had taken payment. The hotel charges were outrageous, so we reckon the round should have been at least eighty quid!

When I settled the bill in the morning, there was £25 car parking charge, (for ONE night) which I refuted, as at no time had anyone mentioned there was a cost. They credited the charge and I paid the bill. When I returned home, I thought "karma" as I'd left a very expensive white shirt at the hotel, I reckon it had gone unnoticed against the white bedlinen when I was packing. I called the Balmoral, and spoke to housekeeping, who said they would look into it. A fortnight later, I received a jiffy bag with my crumpled up shirt in it. I was glad to get my shirt back of course, but thought that such a prestigious hotel would have laundered it before sending, for all it would cost them. That's what I would have done, maybe I expected too much.

May 2009 Elite Club – Dubrovnik, Croatia.

The hotel, The Rixos Palace, as usual was first class, but oddly, the entrance was at the top, and the rest of the hotel went down towards the sea.

Hotel Rixos Palace

One of the most memorable restaurants I've ever been in, was inside the actual wall of the old town, the window overlooking the Adriatic Sea. The food was great, and the atmosphere set the stage for a most enjoyable evening.

*Fantastic dining in the old
City wall...*

The following day we had the choice of a countryside bicycle run, or abseiling down the old city walls. Being a bit of a thrill seeker, I chose the abseiling. Alas, this was subsequently cancelled as the found a crack in the wall. Off to the pub instead then, sod that cycling lark, far too healthy and energetic! On the final day we were taken to the marina, where we split into groups, and boarded sailing yachts. We then headed out into the Adriatic, each getting a shot of being Skipper. Great, I wasn't seasick very much!

All at sea with one of the groups

The usual presentation by Chris Kelly, with Sophie Tirrell in the background...

Another memorable trip over, time to go home...

May 2009 Shawfield Greyhound Stadium.

We had won a performance award from Bentley, for which the prize was £1,000 of vouchers, which I could spend on various things in the High Street. I thought it only fair to share the prize with the team, so approached Bentley to see if they would pay for a team activity, which they did, and sent payment to head office, which I turned into cash.

I thought to do something different, bearing in mind that £1,000 doesn't go that far when there are over 20 of us. Shawfield dog track did hospitality evenings, which fitted the budget, and no one had ever been to greyhound racing before. It was a bit rough and ready, but good fun. Our hospitality got us a three course dinner, couple of drinks, and a £5 bet.

We all had a good laugh, but would we do it again? Doubtful….

June 2010 Elite Club – Cape Town, South Africa.

Myself and all the others who had won a place for the trip in 2010 were asked to vote on which they would prefer to attend. The classic car Grand Prix in Monaco, or the football Word cup in South Africa to watch Englandshire getting beat (Oops!)

Guess what? As the only Scotsman, I was outvoted and we went to South Africa.

Steve Graham one of our Bentley hosts on the left I Don't know who the scruffy guy on the right is!

We were housed in the 5 star Cape Royal Luxury Suites, where I would be sharing a suite with Pericles Bilalis, a lovely wee guy who was the aftersales manager with Bentley Athens. We of course had our own rooms, sharing only the lounge area and kitchen, although why on earth would we be cooking anything in such an opulent setting!

I need to mention a chap, I believe "Juju" was his name, looked after us while we were in the hospitality suite of the football stadium. Not sure what age he would be, fairly young, but had a smile that would brighten any room. He would run after us, fetching drinks, and I remember him asking "one brick of ice or two in your whisky Mr Peter?" He got the equivalent of a £20 tip, and I thought he was going to erupt! Guess that would be a months wages for him, such was the poverty in certain areas of Cape Town.

Left to Right:
Myself, Jay from Jack Barclays,
and Juju on the right

Later evenings were spent on the rooftop of our hotel. One of the Cape Town Bentley owners had paid to take over the full rooftop as hospitality for his customers, draining the two swimming pools and installing massive televisions to watch the world cup on. The whole area was covered over in case of rain. Comfy couches were in abundance, as were complimentary drinks, and we had full access to this during our stay courtesy of the Bentley Aftersales manager in Cape town, who organised it for us.

Getting pissed on the Hotel rooftop...

We had several excursions laid on, going to Cape Point, where the Atlantic and the Indian oceans meet, visiting a colony of penguins (boy did they stink!), a trip to the top of table mountain, and last but not least, a boat to Robben Island, where Nelson Mandela was imprisoned

Yours truly in the jail cell that imprisoned Nelson Mandela

Some of the squad on Robben Island

The obligatory presentation of the certificate for the dealership, being presented by Steve Graham,
the head of Bentley Aftersales at that
time...

I remember getting up at 6.00am the day of our departure, to go look out some souvenirs to take home. I managed to find a shop that sold "vuvuzelas" which, if you remember, were those really annoying trumpet like things that emitted a monotonous monotone, which everyone attending the football matches insisted on blowing! Having procured the souvenirs, I had time for one last wander around Cape Town. The only activity were the poor native workers, cleaning the streets, using makeshift equipment made out of old oil cans. A sign of the poverty which the tourists were to rarely see during the world cup.

Anyway, time to go home...a pretty long flight ahead of me...

June 29th 2010 – Bentley golf tournament at Strathaven Golf Course

This was going to be my first customer golf event, having recently taken up golf again. Did alright considering...

Myself on the right with my good friend "Big Mal" second from the left.

October 2010 – Paris Motor Show.
Myself and my colleague John Cherry from Bentley Edinburgh took the train from Glasgow to London, I had booked sleeper tickets, or so I thought. Turned out the were just reclining seats. No matter, I had brought a half bottle of good malt Whisky which eased the journey somewhat.
We met up with delegates from the other UK dealerships in St Pancras station, and boarded the Eurostar bound for Paris. This was the first time

I'd been through the channel tunnel.

My good friend and fellow aftersales manager from Bentley Newcastle, Jimmy Ellis, proceeded to do the host with the most, having brought two bottles of Buckfast tonic wine, which he, acting like an experienced cabin crew member, made sure we all had a drink, walking up and down the aisle, topping everyone up...

Jimmy Ellis, my good friend and Aftersales Manager from Bentley Newcastle at the time, with his much prized "Bucky"

Most of us had never sampled the brew, and I for one will never again! Vile concoction, but I guess it's just a matter of taste!

We had a free afternoon, so the usual shower of reprobates spent the time drinking beer in a little pavement Cafe, it was so funny, over the few hours we were there, watching the "touch parking" attempts…. Boy do these Frenchies not give a damn!

Left to right: Neil Sawyers (Harwoods Bentley)
John Cherry (Bentley Edinburgh), Jimmy Ellis (Bentley Newcastle)
Marc Frederick (Bentley Leeds), Richard Welch (Bentley Cardiff)
and yours truly. Photo by Kevin Rogan, (Bentley Belfast)

Sadly the only two left with the Bentley dealer network are Neil and Marc, the rest of us have taken different paths for one reason or another.

The Paris motor show was amazing….

Yours truly outside the
Paris Motor Show

We were invited behind the scenes on the Bentley stand, and were led into a small room where we donned headphones and listened to various exhaust sounds, and invited to score them on our personal preferences. This as it turned out was market research for the exhaust tuning on the shortly to be announced Continental GT V8.

Could have done with spending another day there, but time had come to get back on the coach, and a lovely dinner laid on in a typical French Restaurant. The service was also to be typical French, it took an eternity, causing us to run very late for the waiting coach to take us back to the hotel. The coach driver must have been on a promise as he sped at what seemed like 80mph though the Paris Streets.

No time for photographs, but I insisted to the driver we stop, just for two minutes, so I could at least get a picture of me with the Eiffel tower! He grudgingly agreed, and the photo was taken.

Myself and the Eiffel Tower (or was it Blackpool?)

The following morning, the coach was waiting outside the hotel to take us to the station. No sign of John Cherry…....It turned out at breakfast, he had shaken the tomato sauce bottle, not checking if the lid was on tightly. He covered himself and a nearby Frenchman in sauce, and had to rush back to his room to shower and change. (Johns room that is, not the Frenchmans, who was understandably a trifle upset!)

John has to this day never lived that down, and still has the nickname of "Ketchup".

2011 - We didn't qualify for the Elite Club – bummer!

March 2011 – Dealer Conference/Chris Kelly leaving do….
(Down in Englandshire somewhere)

Yours truly presenting Chris Kelly with framed Bentley Glasgow boxer shorts

Some of the "Delegates" a wee bit worse for wear!

Left to Right:
Barry Hopkinson
Kevin Mountford
Myself
Jimmy Ellis
Neil Sawyers

John Ketchup
Cherry catching
up on the
course notes...

July 2011 – Snooker at the Kelvin Hall.

My good friend, golf partner and customer, Malcolm Clark (Big Mal) kindly invited me to a snooker event at the Kelvin Hall in Glasgow. We had VIP passes, as Mal was a close friend of Dennis Taylor, who I had the privilege of meeting, along with Jimmy White, John Parrot, John Virgo, Cliff Thorburn, and last but not least, Michaela Tabb, the gorgeous snooker referee, who in 2009 was the first woman to officiate at world snooker championship final.. I have my picture taken with them all, and they signed my souvenir programme. There followed some exhibition snooker – what a fantastic evening.

Myself with Michaela Tabb

Big Mal with John Parrott

August 2012 Elite Club - Iceland then London for the Olympic Games.

I had to fly from Glasgow to London, and met up with the rest of the "delegates", then from London, we all flew to Iceland, then by coach to the Borg hotel in Reykjavik.

Outside the Borg hotel, which was our home whilst in Reykjavik.

What was laid on the next day was amazing. After breakfast, we all boarded several of those "Superjeeps" and headed for the Langjokul glacier. I was sitting up front due to my reputation for being car sick...best seat in the house apart from the driving seat.

After a while, we reached the bottom of the glacier, where the driver let the tyres down to about 3psi, which gave us the grip needed to climb the icy terrain. Once at the snow covered top, we were given protective overalls, and a snowmobile for each pair of us. As usual, Neil and I paired up. After a quick instruction, we mounted ours, myself taking first turn of driving.

Now, the guys that drive these things in the movies make it look so easy, believe me, the are not! I turned to head off, the front ski went into a glacial crack, and the fucking thing fell over, breaking it in the process. After a change of "skidoo" (and Neil's underwear), we set off.

Soon time to head back, so back into the Jeeps. Down the glacier, then once on the road, the driver pumped the tyres back up with the on board air compressor. On the way back, we went off road, through rivers, and generally had a whale of a time.

Speaking of whales, next day we went whale watching, and all the touristy things. At dinner, we sampled whale meat which was *bowfing, made palatable only by the sauce that accompanied it. Anyway, enough about Iceland, although I could go on, but hey, that would be deviating from the essence of the book. If you want to know about Iceland, go there, or buy a fekking tourist guide book! Lol

*"Bowfing" according to the Oxford English dictionary means Foul Smelling, stinking, unpleasant and horrible.

Me dwarfed by the "Jeep"

The group shot...

Myself and Neil Sawyers

On the Langjokull glacier with our transport for the day

Just before I fell off and broke it!

Wee bit of excitement in the river

After a hard day at the office!

After Iceland, we flew to London, and stayed at the Comfort Inn, in Vauxhall, our evening meal was fish and chips with mushy peas at a top award winning restaurant called "The Dove". Next day after breakfast, we all headed to Olympic park by public transport. What a task for the girls from Noble Events, keeping us all together! We all had been given white Bentley hats, so no doubt that helped….we went by underground from Vauxhall to Kings Cross, walked from there to St Pancras, then by train to Stratford International.

Penny Noble in the centre, talking to Pericles Bilalis from Bentley Athens

Myself and Neil at the Olympic stadium

It certainly was an experience, probably the one and only time I'll ever be at a live Olympic event.

I believe it was in 2012 that we didn't qualify for the 2013 trip. I fell out with Bentley big time over this. As usual, I waited until almost the last minute to submit my final parts order for the year, after carefully checking and double checking order dates and delivery times. We were only about £10,000 short of target, so a normal stock order would take us just over, and was duly submitted.

Half the order was delivered and invoiced between Christmas and New Year, the other half wasn't delivered and invoiced until the 5th of January, making us around £5,000 short – no trip! I was raging to say the least, and no amount of appealing and proving order dates cut any ice. At one of the subsequent meetings at Crewe, I had expressed once again my disgust, and was offered a "bribe" of a set of alloy wheels (not for me personally, but for our dealership) if I stopped mentioning it. I refused, as my principles would not allow me to lower myself to accept.

After this, I lost focus and interest in any further trips.

October 2012 - Golf event at Loch Lomond Golf Club.

My good friend Karl Shirley in the locker room at Loch Lomond Golf Club

Yours truly on the course

August 2013 – Golf at the Carrick.

Not a Bentley or dealer event, just some golf with good friends from the factory and from Bentley Edinburgh. The Englishmen won, and duly earned the "See You Jimmy" wig and bunnet I furnished as prizes. If we had won, they were still getting the prizes! We played again the following year, and they won Justin Bieber calendars each.

Left to Right -
Terry Lee - Bentley Crewe
Karl Shirley – Bentley Crewe
Myself – Bentley Glasgow
John Cherry – Bentley Edinburgh

Terry and Karl wearing their awards

October 2013 – Bentley team building with bodyshop partners.

This was a laugh, particularly the Ferret racing and the dog obedience training, along with archery, shooting, and birds of prey. I forget about what was in the course, I mostly remember running around a field with a sausage on a stick, trying to get a doggie to go around an obstacle course. I dropped my sausage near the beginning, so that was the end of that!

April 2014 – UK Regional Conference at Coombe Abbey

Don't remember much about that one, other than we had a medieval banquet and copious amounts of alcohol.

June 2014 – Carfest at Saint Vincents Hospice.

I was approached by a good friend Willie Chrystal (total petrolhead). Willie owned the company that did all our Health and Safety, Fire and First Aid Training. He was organising a "Carfest" to raise funds for St Vincents Hospice, in Johnstone, near his home town of Paisley. I would be delighted, and myself and Ian McFadyen took two Bentleys, with a third one supplied by a customer and pal of Willies. It was a great success, I had brought several items, model Bentleys, Bentley umbrellas and the like as raffle prizes. We did the same for a few years, but the Carfest got too big for the available space at the Hospice, so it was moved to Paisley town centre. Afraid it lost some of it's charm. I don't know if Park's do it any more now that I'm no longer there.

Part of the Bentley display

Ian McFadyen, the oldest swinger in town!

June 2014 – Worldwide dealer conference in Manchester.

I reckon this was the first time I had met Fred Sirieix, who was brought in by Bentley to assist with the customer experience and how to improve it. Of course he was nicknamed "Freddie the Frog", don't know who came up with that, probably Neil Sawyers!

"Freddie the Frog" with us at Manchester United Stadium

Fred was at the time, general manager of the Michelin starred "Galvin at Windows" restaurant in London, and had a reputation for customer excellence. He had a few good ideas, and like myself, disagreed with videoing customer car faults and sending to the customer. To him and I, this showed a lack of trust between dealer and customer, having to justify any work required. It did have it's uses however, I used it to keep customers advised on how the repairs were going, but only if they expressed an interest. A good example would be removing an engine, which allayed their fears when they saw how professional we were. Anyway, once more I digress!

The next time I was at the factory, I asked where Fred was, and was told he was too expensive, having previously costing around £1,000 per day, but now he had grown a beard and was on the telly, it went up to £25,000 per day! (allegedly)

Fred is pretty famous now, hosting and appearing in numerous programmes. Nice guy, good luck to him.

What a great time was had by all. We stayed in the Hilton in Manchester, and had a VIP tour of Manchester United Football Stadium, and as much as I don't appreciate football, it was certainly a most enjoyable experience.

After the conference, we were taken to a converted church where lavish entertainment and dinner were laid on. As I have said, Bentley don't do things by halves.

It was great to catch up with a lot of friends from many countries who I have met over the years.

John (Ketchup) Cherry posing at his favourite condiment at Manchester Stadium

On the Right:
A motley crew, some from Bentley
and some from the dealer network
Many, including myself have moved on to pastures new....

Left to Right:
John (Ketchup) Cherry
Harald Perko– Bentley
Vienna
Neil Sawyers – Harwoods
Bentley

My good friend Neil
Sawyers posing in the
trophy room at
Manchester United

Myself and Pericles Bilalis,
Aftersales Manager from
Bentley Athens

July 2014 – Welcome to McLaren.

As the "new boys" to the McLaren scene, it was mandatory to attend the welcome training course at the factory, the McLaren Technology Centre (MTC) in Woking, Englandshire.

We stayed in a very pleasant hotel for four nights, where all of the classroom sessions took place. It was a total immersion in McLaren history, a lot of it interactive, never boring as these sessions can sometimes be.

The MTC was amazing, and we met a guy named Neil Trundle, whose job it was to look after the incredibly vast array of historical McLarens, ensuring every one was a running example. What an interesting guy he was...he was the lead technician for the McLaren race team a number of years ago in the glory years, and had some great stories to relate.

One thing I found ridiculous was the lack of cigarette (Marlborough) advertising on the historical race cars. Government legislation didn't allow it, even on heritage and museum cars. Bloody ridiculous, no common sense. They were a piece of history, and should be kept as such. Rant over! All the staff were dressed immaculately in the corporate outfits, except for one group who were just wearing casual gear, jackets draped over the back of chairs, and generally looking scruffy! I asked our tour guide why the exception, and got the reply that Ron Dennis was not due in today, so they thought they could get away with it. Guess who we bumped into on our way out? Yup, Ron Dennis with a group of Chinese businessmen. I shudder to think of the repercussions! Ron Dennis was well known to be totally OCD, and judging by the intricate detail our showroom had to be, I could believe everything we had heard.

The time came for the bit I was really looking forward to....driving the cars around Thruxton Race track...AWESOME! The cars were fantastic...

Yours truly about to drive the 650S
Note the race suit and boots....

Some of the guys after the tour of MTC

I met a great bunch of people, two were from Paris and spoke no English. We had a right laugh in the evenings using Google Translate on our phones. I taught them a few Scottish words as one does in these situations.

One evening there was a barbecue laid on for us in the hotel, and we all got on great, assisted by copious amounts of beer.

The full worldwide training group. I keep in touch with a few of them on Facebook

Getting my Welcome to McLaren Certificate

February 20th 2015 Bentley Awards Grand Ball – London

We got the train from Glasgow Central, and the seats were not together due to my ineptness in booking them. We tried to amend them at Glasgow Central station, but a jobsworth at the ticket office couldn't do anything, unless we bought first class tickets costing a fortune, which we refused.

A guy who worked in the station wearing a hi-viz jacket came up to us and asked what the problem was, as Eleanor was a bit upset. I told him the tale, he said "hold on a minute sir" and went and spoke to his manager. He then came back and told us to go to the first class carriage, and the first table on the right is ours, free of charge. I couldn't believe our luck, shook his hand and bunged him twenty quid. We had made up sandwiches and stuff for the journey, which were now no longer required, as drinks and meals were all included. Tried it on the return journey, but no success. Still, one out of two ain't bad! It was to be a very lavish affair, Neil McCallum got one of the awards, so we didn't go away empty handed.

*Pre Award
Drinkie-Poos*

*Myself   and
Eleanor
looking at the
table plan, hoping
not to be sat next
to any numpties!*

*From the left:
Myself, Vicky Street,
Bentley customer relations co ordinator
and Neil McCallum*

We stayed on in London for another three nights, albeit at a lesser hotel where we got three nights bed and breakfast for less than one night in the other hotel.

March 18th and May 15th 2015 – Factory visit with Aftersales customers.

We were allocated a number of slots for factory tours, so it was decided to include aftersales customers as a reward for their loyal custom. These visits were usually reserved for sales customers and prospects.

In March, we took two cars and drove some customers to the factory. Myself and Jim Ross did the driving. In May, I took three customers. These visits went down exceptionally well, and still often talked about.

Above - March 18th 2015

Getting a history lesson from the tour guide.

Above - Left to right on March 18th 2015:
Aiden Weir, Ian Weir, Robert Daniel, Billy Tennant,
Gerry Begley, Jim Ross (Our driver) and myself

Above - left to right on May 15th 2015:
Our guide, with Alan Campbell, David McLeod and Barry Wood.

June 2015 – Golf Event at Loch Lomond.

The day started off by taking the GT3r and parking it along with our other cars, in front of the clubhouse. When I say clubhouse, more like a stately home. Breakfast was fabulous, setting me up for what was to be quite a long day. These were always very daunting affairs, I'm afraid I don't take golf that seriously, although I do enjoy playing. I remember being first to tee off at the very exclusive Loch Lomond golf club, with everyone watching, and more by luck than skill, I hit not too bad a shot. Probably the one and only good shot! After 9 holes, lunch served up in the manner befitting such a magnificent setting.

I didn't win, well, it wouldn't be politically correct to beat any customers to a trophy!

After a magnificent dinner, the prizes were awarded, and it was time to head home. As it was getting late, I was to take the GT3r home with me. Where I live, is virtually in the Clyde valley, and that road is home to numerous garden centres, the patrons of which usually dawdle along the road from one garden centre to another, spoiling what is a very decent drivable road.

This was after eight o'clock on a beautiful summer evening, and there was hardly another car in sight. I put the windows down, selected sport mode, and lets just say the car performed and sounded fantastic, one of the most enjoyable drives I've had in ages.

The Bentley GT3r - One of my top three Bentleys of all time...

Yours truly with the real GT3 race car...

The Continental GT3r road version sitting outside my house

12th July 2015 Hawkstone Golf Weekend

This wasn't a company event, just a few friends getting together for a golfing weekend. Karl had booked the hotel, which was dinner, bed and breakfast, and a round of golf on each of the two championship courses.

I had brought with me five "Art of Service" awards, which I had previously made, using some white Bentley boxes, to which I had stuck copies of the Art of Service title sheets. Now, the Art of Service was a game thought up by Bentley, (based on an idea by Fred Sirieix who is mentioned earlier in this book) to which everyone in the dealership had to play, and prove by photographs or video that they did actually play. This involved taking technicians, sales guys, in fact everyone off their jobs to play the game on product knowledge. This was a standing joke in the dealer network, although the automatic issue at a cost of £600 was no joke. Most dealers just played lip service, but anyway, I digress. I had gone to the pound shop, and bought 5 of the silliest games they had, which I put into the boxes, and gave out to the guys at the end of the weekend as prizes.

We had a great weekend, good food, good drink and fantastic company.

Left to right:

Terry Lee
Karl Shirley
Jimmy Ellis
Neil Sawyers
Dom Cooper
Myself

The award ceremony, complete with the "Art of Service"

November 2015 – Bentayga launch, Club Marbella

See chapter on New Model Launches.

February 2017 – Dealer Conference, Gleneagles.

This was to be a fantastic night, the entertainment turned out to be none other than the Red Hot Chilli Pipers. We had a table right next to the stage, couldnie be better!

Eleanor and myself, ready for the "do"

June 2017 – McLaren World dealer meeting in Spain.

I flew to Barcelona airport, where I met up with Charlotte, who was the aftersales manager with McLaren Ascot at the time. We were taken to a great hotel in Sitges, Southwest of Barcelona itself.

I met some great people from all over the world, and mostly played pool in the bar...tough job!

February 2018 – Bentley Grand Ball, London.

Every year, Bentley would hold an event to thank dealers and make some awards, this time we stayed in the Corinthia Hotel in London. A very grand hotel, but due to a double booking, there was a fashion award ceremony held that night in the hotel. Bentleys "do" was relegated to a hotel two doors down, no hardship, still a top hotel. Once the awards were over, some of us went back to the Corinthia for a drink, and that's when we met WILL.I.AM, of Black Eyed Peas and the Voice fame. Lovely guy, had a selfie and a handshake with him and my wife Eleanor got a cuddle.

Yours Truly with my new best riend…….
WILL.I.AM

After paying for a round of drinks in the Corinthia, taking out a second mortgage, we returned to our function hotel where the drinks were free. Who said Scots were mean?

2013, 2014, 2015, 2016, and 2017 we didn't qualify for the Elite Club, and when they announced that partners would be included in the trips, I thought it selfish to exclude my wife Eleanor for the sake of my stubbornness! It was also rumoured that this would be the last Elite club trip, so full steam ahead, and won a place in 2018 to Italy, the Amalfi coast with our partners.

I'm glad I had put my gripe to one side, as this was to be one of the best trips ever. As it happens, there was to be one further trip, but I had retired by then, plus this Covid pandemic   put paid to any trips actually taking place.

Anyway, back to the Amalfi trip on the 18th to the 21st of May...

May 2018 Elite Club – Amalfi Coast, Italy.

What a stunning location, the hotel was halfway up the cliff face, and we had an outstanding room with balcony overlooking the coast. Bentley had some phenomenal excursions and cuisine laid on for us. Bring it on! What an outstanding amount was crammed into that weekend…..

After the arrival welcome, we had drinks followed by dinner. I was talked into eating Octopus by Steve O'Hara from Bentley, and as it was after a few "refreshments" I reluctantly agree to try it. I had second helpings… it was delicious! I had previously gone off seafood since I had crabs, but that's another story!

The day following our arrival, we had a yacht excursion to Sorrento, where we had ice cream before getting a coach back to the hotel, followed by drinks and dinner.

On day 3, Sunday, a power boat excursion to the isle of Capri, where we had the choice so sunbathe by the pool, or get taxis into the town. We chose the former. Our skipper was a character and a half, serenading us most of the trip with a rather fine operatic voice, and keeping us topped up with beer and Prosecco!

The last evening was to an ancient Abbey, where we were all presented with our dealership certificates. When called up for mine, I ran and jumped up, kicking my heels in the air. Once I had the certificate, Steve from Bentley asked me to do it again, this time for the camera. That photograph made it into the beautiful book we we given on our return to the UK.

The presentation…
Jonathan Morris, Myself and Steve O'Hara

No too bad for an auld yin!

Monday, day 4 came all too soon. As there was most of the day to kill before our return flights, we visited Pompeii, which was fantastic, although maybe just a wee bit "touristy". I particularly remember the ancient brothel, with its rather racy pictures still painted on the walls. Wonder what kind of broth they sold in those days…..

This was followed by lunch and a tour of a local vineyard…….then homeward bound with some great memories that will stay with us for the rest of our lives.

Myself and my good lady Eleanor on the last night overlooking the bay.

November 2018 Royal Yacht Britannia.

Gavin had organised a customer event, and to be a bit different from the usual, was to be in the Royal Yacht Britannia. I tried to book a hotel in Edinburgh, but as there was a major rugby match on at Murrayfield, there was nowhere to be had. Didn't fancy driving home after what would be a complimentary drink evening!

I remembered a chap called Derek Mowatt, whom I've done business with before, and a genuinely nice guy. I seemed to remember he owned a hotel. A call later and he had managed to get me a room, not the biggest, but hey, it was only for the night...sorted!

Myself and wife Eleanor took a Bentley through, for display outside the Royal yacht. It was a black tie affair, and what a night it was. We got a tour of the ship, dinner was magnificent, and Her Majesty the Queens own sitting room was opened up, normally cordoned off to the public. I sat in a chair that no doubt the queen had parked her royal backside on! My good friend, Tim Hodgson, did the after dinner speech, reminiscing about his time in the factory.....most enjoyable. I always tried to get Tim to speak "Scots" every time I saw him....favourite phrase was "ye cannae get a jeelie piece in Glesca Green", and "I'll gie ye wan wi ra heid pal!"

We had a brilliant night, great customers and company. Got a taxi back to the hotel, then another to the yacht in the morning to collect the Bentley. All on expenses...woo hoo!

Left: Myself and Eleanor in the formal dining room... (Note my empty glass!)

Right: Her Majesties sitting room.

139

This was going to be my final "Jolly", as I retired on the 4th of February the following year.

 The chapter on "The Jollies", wouldn't be complete without mentioning Penny Noble, MD of Nobel Events Limited. Penny and her fabulous team organised most, if not all of the Elite club events and dealer conferences Etc. I remember her girls leading some 20 of us through a busy London, taking trains and undergrounds to reach the Olympic Stadium, not losing a single person. We did all have on a white Bentley baseball cap to separate us from the crowds. Some feat to be sure......

Chapter Ten - Some memorable customers, the good, the bad and the ugly.

I've met some great customers in my time, but this chapter will focus on the more interesting ones.....some names have been changed to protect the guilty!

In the days of Springkell Avenue, the customer reception was also the boss's office. Customers just drove into the workshop...never was a good idea!

I remember early on in my career, the sales guys had sold a Rover 2000 to an elderly Jewish gentleman. When he came to collect it, refused to take it as the car had a German "Kienzel" clock, and he point blank refused to take delivery unless something was done. No doubt the atrocities suffered to the Jews by the Germans in WW2 had a bearing on his refusal. We managed to acquire a "Smiths" clock, which was duly fitted, and resulted in a happy customer.

There was one owner, a chap called Nino Verrico* with a white Shadow Mulliner Park Ward 2 door, who, for whatever reason was not happy, stormed out the boss's office, jumped into his car and wheel spinned out the workshop. He had, however, forgotten that he had left his briefcase at the rear of the car, having meant to put it in the boot – result was he drove right over the case, sending his papers etc. flying all over the workshop...oh how we all laughed!

Another time, that same customer accidentally selected the wrong gear and pinned one of the mechanics against the workshop heater.....think he settled out of court with that one! The lad he hit didn't have much luck, someone let a ramp down on his foot, but what made it worse, contrary to what you might think, was that he had steel toecap safety boots on. This had the effect of crushing the cap onto his toes, but rather than when the ramp was raised, hopefully relieving the pressure, the steel toecap remained squashed onto his foot. The boot had to be cut off at A & E!!

* I still keep in contact with Nino, and he is quite happy to be mentioned by name, he thought it would be a laugh...

The late Jimmy Logan, the Scottish entertainer and comedian had a Silver Cloud. He was more famous at that time for a TV advertisement for Simmers Country Perkins biscuits, and the catchphrase was

"Luvvly Biscuits, luvvly luvvly biscuits". As he walked up the workshop to the reception, around eight heads popped out from under cars, and chorused "Luvvly biscuits, luvvly luvvly biscuits"

He was not amused, and stormed out! For a comedian, not much of a sense of humour!

Another customer was the singer Moira Anderson, famous for singing, among others "For These are my Mountains". Similar scenario, she was walking up the workshop, and again, around eight heads popped out and chorused "For These are my Mountains"!

She burst out laughing, for a singer, she had a great sense of humour!

We had rather flamboyant customer, Terry Alvis, who was the owner of a nightclub called "Blazes" in Charing Cross, and had the latest Shadow 2 at the time, with the registration number TER 177, but spaced out to read TER1 77. As I say, he was a flamboyant character, some six foot two, long dark hair, and wore an ankle length mink coat (The Glasgow version of Peter Stringfellow!) I had to give him a lift back to his office at Charing cross, so I brought the bosses Morris Marina round, and picked him up. Now in those days, it was not frowned upon to smoke, indeed, it was very fashionable (or so I thought). I lit up a cigarette, and smoked it while driving him into town. Now, changing gear with my "fag" in my left hand, I accidentally stubbed it out on his mink coat – thankfully he never noticed, and I promptly threw what was left of the ciggy out the window.

He had purchased Lee Castle, in the Clyde Valley, and with it came the title of the 33rd Baron of Lee, so he now became Baron Terence Alvis of Lee. A fitting title. I remember once dropping his Shadow back to the castle, and Terry came to the rather impressive huge oak front door. I said "Terry, some place you've got here" to which he replied "It'll be ok once I've built the extension for the kids". He than thanked me and gave me a bottle of whisky, which was labelled "Terrys Elite", I thought in my young mind, how cool is that? Through a search on Linkedin, he is now seemingly going strong as a retired chairman in a Cape Town Organisation. I wish him well, he was a character.

Lee Castle was to feature again with a new owner later on ……

Another memorable customer was a chap called Jimmy Glasgow, who at the time owned Crosmyloof ice rink, along with many other businesses. I was still young, and didn't have much to do with him, that is, until I had RRS. He had four Rolls-Royces, a long wheelbase Shadow registration number AXS 9, another Shadow, GHS 45N, a Silver Shadow 2, KGE808V, and a Silver Cloud which I never saw. One day, he phoned me up, having been recommended by another customer, and asked If I would be interested in taking on GHS45N, which had been set on fire and lay in a garage for years. I went to inspect the car, someone obviously had a grudge and set the front tyre on fire, causing a great deal of damage to the suspension, paintwork, engine bay and all rubber components.

I was always hungry for work and took the job on. I sourced a lot of the parts second hand to save costs, and any time I needed more cash in advance, it wasn't a problem. I always remember going to his office in the town centre, where he would sit behind a big oak desk, and would write me out a cheque.

That job took several months off and on, but I got there in the end. AXS 9 was sold, and subsequently in an accident, and I also got that repair to do. KGE808V unfortunately met with a sad ending, left in the open garage at Mr Glasgows house in Bridge of Weir and just rotted away.

KGE808V looking rather sorry for itself....

 I don't know where it is now, but Mr G had been put in a home, and that was that. Presumably he is no more, and his magnificent, albeit old house is now demolished, to make way for flats. Sad...

One of the bedrooms in the old house...

We had another quite flamboyant young customer named
*Pete McFadden, who owned a beautiful Le-Mans blue Silver Shadow with a white Everflex roof. When he dropped off his car, I would run him into a multi story car park in the town, where he would pick up his old Ford Fiesta, which he used to conduct his business, which was I believe in the pharmaceutical industry, and couldn't be seen driving a Rolls-Royce. He also owned a beautiful hotel next to Queens Park.

* Name has been changed to protect the guilty!

Another young customer with a Shadow was Eric Rowan, nice guy, and had, at the time a stunning music system installed in his Silver Shadow. I had never seen the like before, with a graphic equaliser and a wonderful echo facility, fantastic! He also kept in his glove box, a trophy inscribed - "Awarded to Eric Rowan, best kisser in Minskys". Minskys was one of the many night clubs in Glasgow, where we all used to frequent in the late Seventies and Eighties.

My boss Big John one day told me about this insomniac customer, who had bought a new Silver Shadow 2. At night, unable to sleep, he would go to his garage, and with the help of a halogen spotlight, go over every inch of paintwork on the car. He would then bring the car in for rectification. Nine times out of ten, there was nothing visible with the paintwork, glad I didn't have to deal with him. With the best will in the world, these cars were painted by humans, and somebody with eagle eyes could always pick a fault!
Back in the day, a Silver Shadow would command a premium, so much so, you could keep a new car for 6 months, then trade it in for a new car, getting back what was originally paid, if not more.
One particular customer would have a standing order for a new car ever 6 months, in the end getting bored with the more run of the mill colours and ordering one in bright Pink, with a white everflex roof and whitewall tyres. Got to say, it did look stunning! This same customer also ordered a new Phantom VI limousine, in bright Le Mans Blue, and it had, the first I'd ever seen, a colour television in the rear compartment.
I used to collect the Bentley of Mr John Stenhouse, and take him to his beautiful yacht berthed in the Inverkip Marina. I always have him a hand with his luggage, and always admired his yacht, which was one of the classic motor yachts, which looked like it dated back to the 1930's, I really

don't know, but it was stunning. Mr Stenhouse subsequently bought a new Silver Shadow 2, Red Badge 75th Anniversary model, one of only 75 produced to commemorate the 75th Anniversary of Rolls-Royce.

It was finished in Shell Grey coachwork, and Mr Stenhouse proceeded to smash it to such an extent, it had to be returned to the factory for repair. Sorry to say, the car was never right after that, always exhibiting an annoying wind noise.

Mrs Penman had a Silver Shadow, registration number HF6, with coachwork in Silver Sand, spoiled, in my opinion, by the pure white interior leather. Any time I delivered the car after service, Mrs Penman was usually out in her garden at the house in Newlands, and she would always give me a rose... lovely lady, long since gone.

Speaking of white interiors, when at Gaulds, a customer ordered a new Silver Spirit, in a unique colour called "Plum Crazy with Violet". The interior was in white leather. Rolls-Royce did something they very rarely do, and that was to refuse to supply the car with a pure white dash and top roll. To keep the owner happy, we removed the dash trim and recoloured it in white, much against our better judgment, as anyone who has ever placed a newspaper on top of their dash will testify, when the sunlight hits it, the effect is to dazzle the driver. The customer was well warned before we carried this out. We also fitted a rear spoiler from a Ford Granada to the boot lid….Hmmmmmm…

Still, his motorcar and up to him what he does with it.

When the time came he traded it back into us, and the car had to go to London, where these things are more acceptable, as nobody here would look at it!

I first met a chap called David McLeod in the RRS in Hillington days. He was introduced to me by his wife Maureen, who was a back up driver on my wedding car business, driving her Mercedes. David was and still is an avid classic car buff, and over the years gave us a great many repairs and restorations to carry out for him.

One time, David called me up to go and inspect a 1950's Rolls-Royce Silver Dawn for him. Problem was it was in Germany, so a flight was organised, and I met at the airport by the car owner, a Mr Claus Erbrecht. He took me to a town called Brest, where he owned a run down hotel and was in the process of renovating it.

I inspected the Silver Dawn, which was lying in bits, engine out and stripped, body off the chassis, and in a right old state. I would advise David against this one. As I was flying out the following day, I would be staying in an attic bedroom in the old hotel, but first, we were going to a local pub for a meal. Downside was it was in the next town. Claus dug out two old bicycles, and we peddled to the pub. We had a great night, good food, lots of beer and pool playing. Time to head back, slightly pished. Claus led the way, as we only had one light and it was on his bike!

Next morning, Claus was to run me back to the airport, but he couldn't as he had other commitments. He did write down, however, the exact timings and locations of the bus and two trains I was to get.

I was nervous about being stuck in a foreign country, able to speak no more than schoolboy German (which incidently I failed my "O" level). My fears were unfounded, as everything went exactly to plan, timings were spot on – typical Germans.

David did however, buy the car, but on the understanding that Claus would build it up and drive it back to Scotland, which, several months later he accomplished. Well, I say accomplished, we had a hell of a lot to do to get it anywhere near right. The car is still around, under the registration number KKU5.

David had a beautiful Ferrari Daytona which was on display at the Doune motor museum, and he decided to collect it one Saturday, could I go with him? Gladly, and I got to drive the Daytona back, albeit in the pouring rain. Switch off the wipers David said, and watch what happens. I did, and it was amazing – due to the aerodynamics of the motorcar, hardly a drop of rain touched the screen. Amazing.

Sadly, Davids wife Maureen passed away several years ago, but David is still one of my very good friends, and we often keep in touch.

I have recently encountered Claus Erbrecht, and keep in touch on Facebook.

The Doune motor museum features during the Murray Motor years, when I first met Stephen Henry. Stephen was presented with a stunning new Bentley Continental R for winning the 1994 Embassy World Snooker title. He loved the car, but didn't relish the attention it attracted, especially when onlookers saw who was driving, and the registration number "CUE1" probably didn't help...

It was thought at the time that the motorcar would be an investment, and it was arranged for the car to be on display in the Doune Museum. I met Stephen there, and with the press in attendance, he handed the Bentley keys over to me. We then had a roll and sausage in the cafeteria.

I had arranged that every month, that I would send a technician to the museum, he would put a gallon of petrol in, and take the car for a run. He would check it over and made sure the battery and everything was as it should be. These cars at the time had to be serviced every six months or 6,000 miles, so we would collect the car and carry out the service, just to keep the service history up to date. We did this a few times, then it was realised that these cars were no longer appreciating, so it was taken from the museum, and presumably sold.

What a youthful pair
Myself with Stephen handing over the Bentley keys

Sadly, the Doune Motor Museum was to close its doors on the 30th of November, 1998.

I first met Ian Dennison when we were at Townhead Street, when he bought a 1997/8 Bentley Brooklands, not from us, but from a dealer down South. Ian was a lovely guy, but one of the most fastidious people I have ever met. We looked after him, and tried to make the car as perfect as possible for him, following his (always typed) letters of instruction. The car was regularly serviced by us, it was his pride and joy, until one day, in December 2011, he contacted me, most upset. Someone had run into the car, and it was badly damaged.

When I saw it, I knew right away that it would be written off by the insurance company. I picked Ian up, and took him to our bodyshop, where the car had been recovered to. He Wanted to say goodbye, and remove any of his personal effects. We never saw the car again.

Shortly afterwards, I received a letter from Ian, along with two one-hundred pound notes. He had also sent a similar letter to Ian McFadyen, who I always entrusted to look after the Bentley whenever it was with us. They made very few like Ian Dennison……..

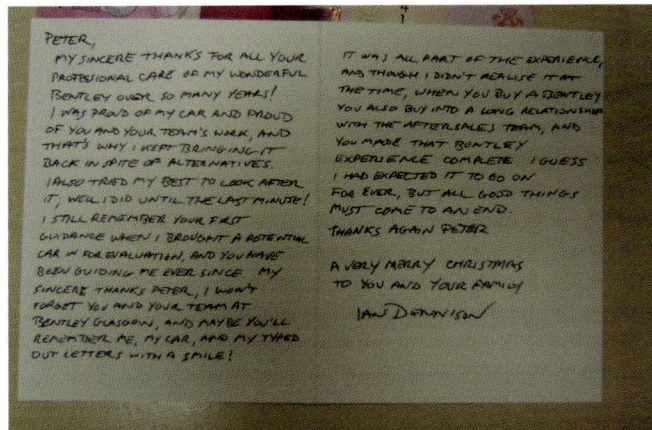

The last letter from Ian Dennison, which I have kept and will treasure

Sad end to a once beautiful motorcar

Lady Weir was one of our owners who had a lovely Bentley T1. Once a year, she would attend Harley Street, why I never knew, but that coincided with her Bentley needing a service. I always had the pleasure of collecting the car in Ayrshire, and running Lady Weir to Glasgow Airport for her to catch the plane to London.

Her car was later sold to another lovely lady, Marjory Matheson. I had the pleasure of looking after that particular car, then onto an anniversary "Red Badge" Silver Shadow 2, mentioned earlier when owned by John Stenhouse, and finally onto her Bentley Turbo R. Mrs Matheson was a bit of a petrol head, I had obtained a lovely Audi TT cabriolet for her, which she sold back to us once some "neds" at a set of traffic lights made a scathing comment to her about age and her car. She also had and regularly drove her Triumph TR6 pretty much up to her passing away.

I was at her thanksgiving service in the Glasgow Cathedral, where it was packed out. She was a very popular lady, and devoted a great deal to charity.

RIP Marjorie Matheson

Not long after RRS Glasgow Ltd was up and running, I had the honour to meet a chap called Alan Caulfield. He drove into the garage when it was in Garrioch Road, with the drivers window stuck down on his Silver Shadow. He had been sent up to me by Brian Lynch at Clyde Valet, at Finnieston, with whom I had a mutual agreement, that is I would recommend them, if they did the same for me. It worked well. Anyway, I gave Alan my Mercedes to go about his business, and at the very least I would get the window back up, if not able to get it working. It was a bad connection inside the door, which was duly fixed. Alan came back, delighted, handing me a couple of bottles of wine, and settling the bill, which wasn't very expensive.

Alan turned out to be a true gentleman, supporting me with all his vehicle maintenance requirements, with RRS. He had progressed onto a Silver Spirit, two tone coachwork, light ocean over deep ocean, which we carried out some paintwork on. He also had a Range Rover, registration number CAU1T, and asked it we could do something to make it a bit special. What about a two-tone to match the Rolls-Royce? Go for it he said, which we did and it looked stunning if I say so myself. He followed me through Murray Motors, then on with Douglas Park.

Sad to say, I was the last person to see Alan alive, we had shaken hands, and he headed for home. His car crashed into a barrier at the end of the M74, and he did not survive. I attended his funeral, there were hundreds there, he was a well respected member of the business community, and will be sadly missed. Alan was only 52 years old, taken far too soon…..

RIP Alan Caulfield

Alan had lived in a country mansion called Glenlora out in Lochwinnoch, stunning location, I visited it regularly, as living in Beith, Ayrshire at the time, I was just 10 minutes away from me.

Glenlora didn't have the best of endings for those that lived there, first with the passing of Alan, then the next owner fell on financial ruin, and the next owner, Louis Woodcock, unfortunately passed away with cancer. I remember very well the day Louis told me he had cancer. He had owed £45 for the MOT on his Bentley continental for several months. Now, I would not dream of chasing a loyal customer over such a paltry amount (head office would disagree!) but one day Louis called me apologising for the tardy payment, and duly settled the amount outstanding. He again apologised, saying he had just come out of hospital, having had his entire left arm and shoulder amputated due to cancer. Wow! The last thing on my mind would have been to settle the bill for £45! While chatting away, he had a sudden thought that I might be able to suggest some form of hand controls for his Bentley, which I duly obliged and subsequently got sorted out for him. Sad to say, Louis passed away not long after…..

His two sons, Daniel and Antony however, continued with their late fathers wish and successfully completed the gruelling 8,000 mile Peking to Paris challenge in 2013, using their dads 1927 Bentley. An account of this is available on YouTube… look for Peking to Paris 2013

RIP Louis Woodcock

One more tragedy to strike Glenlora was in March 2012, when the groundsman was found dead in his car, after suffering a heart attack – he was only 53.

I believe Louis Woodcocks family still live in Glenlora, running it as a successful shooting venue. Good luck to them, hopefully no more misfortunes will ensue.

I first met a rather eccentric chap called "Melvin John Carter Devine the First" around 1996 when he first bought his Rolls-Royce Silver Shadow 2. The car was lovely, with coachwork in Onyx, with a dark brown Everflex roof. Onyx was then a light green, as opposed to the Onyx of today which is close to black.

Melvin was a gambler, and put the registration number "MJI 5050" on the Shadow, standing for his initials Melvin John 1st, and the gambling odds of 50/50. He wanted something a bit different, so the car was refinished in Silver over Red, with a Red Everflex roof. Not to everyones taste, but hey, it was his car. Melvin faithfully had the car serviced, but as the years went by, I could see the signs that Melvin wasn't getting any younger, and did not have the funds available he once had.

He had always left an envelope (some of which I still have) for me when the car was returned, in the beginning usually a twenty pound note, but as time went on, he left anything, including ties, cufflinks, and the last thing he gave me was the dummy cufflinks you get with a new shirt.

It got to the stage we would collect the car, put a gallon of petrol in it, charge the battery, give it a run and drop it back. Never charged him, but he always left a fiver for the petrol.

Melvin sadly passed away a few years ago, and as he didn't have and family, he left the car to a jeweller friend of his.

A year or so later, I got a call from this friend, asking if I knew of anyone who would buy the car. How much? I made an offer and bought the car. More of this later.

I had the honour to meet a gentleman named Basil Lockwood Goose, originally he was Basil Goose, but when he married Joan Lockwood in 1954, Joans father asked Basil if he could keep the Lockwood name alive, as Joan was the last of the family line, hence the double barrel name of Lockwood-Goose was created. Basil retired in 1988, and his well equipped engineering workshop at his home was where he created many projects, one of which was to modify the steering on his beautiful Bentley S3, to give a more responsive feel. Basil was to trade this car in and purchase a Bentley Turbo R from us. Basil was an active member of the RREC, and is sadly missed. He had completely restored five pre-war Rolls-Royces, the last of which was completed just before his death.

A beautiful portrait in oils of Basil Lockwood-Goose

RIP Basil Lockwood-Goose 1929 – 2014

We had a customer with a Bentley Arnage, and believe me when I tell you this guy didn't have a clue how anything on his car worked. I often had to reset his radio push buttons for him, as he couldn't even manage that! One time, I was on holiday, the guy who was covering for me had to do the same, but charged him eighty quid for the privilege. Guess who got an earful from the customer on my return...I did come and go with him a bit eventually...anything for a quiet life, although the same customer at the time of writing had bought several Bentleys from us, which he may not have done if he got pissed off!

I first met Vincent Mothersole when he brought his rather tired Bentley T2 in for some repairs. Addressing him as Mr Mothersole, he said please, call me Vincent. He then proceeded to give me the reason why. His wife had been shopping in Littlewoods previously, and was waiting on being called to collect her order. The assistant had obviously folded the sales ticket across her surname, and announced "would Mrs Ersole (Arsehole) please come and collect her order". I thought he's a lovely bloke, unfortunately his car was one of the ones you would value at £30 per ton! We did however look after him sympathetically, as his wife objected to him having a Bentley, she would rather have a new kitchen!

One day, Vincent came in looking a wee bit flustered and irate. I asked him what was up, to which he replied "these bloody road works on the motorway, the cones are not spaced correctly, someone should get their arse booted for that"! Turns out, before he retired, he was in the roads department of the council. I said that I knew a girl that worked there called Elaine, to which he replied, not sure, what was her surname? Closure, I responded, Elaine Closure….nope he didn't know her! Duhh!

Another time, as you do, we invited him to one of our showroom events for the launch of the new Spur. He turned up with a friend, and somehow managed to collar one of the big wigs from Bentley Motors, and proudly stated that they had got the train as it was cheaper than the petrol the Bentley would use! He got a strange look, and no doubt reinforced the image of the Scots being mean…..

Vincent Mothersole on the Right at the Flying Spur launch

I had said previously that Lee Castle would come up again. By this time, around 2000, the castle was owned by a Canadian, Leslie Peters, who became the 34th Baron of Lee around 1988. One day, there was a telephone call from him, he is looking to purchase a car, could we take some of our stock to show him. We summoned anyone who could drive, and we took several cars to the castle in the Clyde Valley, and lined them up on the castle esplanade. There was a Bentley Arnage, a Jaguar, and from memory a Range Rover and some others. The reason the Arnage and the Jaguar sticks in my memory, is that the Baron instructed us to open the front passenger door on all the cars, and the one his dog went to would be the one he bought! At this point, I wished we had brought some Pedigree Chum to spread on each seat! There wasn't really any need, as the dog, I believe it to be a wire haired Airedale, jumped into the Arnage **AND** the Jaguar! The baron, good as his word, bought them both.

Now, it is said that the Baron was an ex Spitfire pilot during the war, and was shot down and wounded, resulting in both legs being amputated and prosthetics fitted. Whether this is true or not, it's a great story, but I do know his leg mobility was severely limited, in fact he could not bend his legs. This resulted in a bit of an issue, as the Baron would always sit in the rear of the Bentley, his dog having pride of place on a custom tartan seat cover specially commissioned to fit on the front passenger seat. Of course it would be the chauffeur who was driving.

I came up with the idea to wire up the electric front seat to a switch we installed in the rear overhead console, so that the Baron could "park his bum" on the back seat, remotely move the front seat forwards as far as it would go, then he could swing his legs in. The seat was then moved back again, so the dog had plenty of room. The Baron certainly loved that dog.

Moving on to Mr and Mrs Ferguson, who were a lovely couple, very much on in years, and owning a Silver Spirit. They had a holiday home in France, and regularly made the trip in their Spirit. One day, they called in on their way to France (We were just off the M74 motorway) with a strange buzzing noise coming from the car. I sat in the car, and sure enough, heard the buzzing, coming from the left hand side.

I guided the couple to the lounge area, while I checked the car out. I drove the car into the workshop, and switched the car off. Strange, the noise was still there.

I noticed Mrs Fergusons handbag was sitting on the footwell, so I thought I'd take it to her in case she needed anything out of it. Hmmm, the buzzing was coming from her bag! I walked through to the lounge, handbag buzzing, and my mind imagining all sorts. Turned out it was her electric toothbrush!

Several weeks later, the car drives in with the rear suspension dragging, and rock hard. They had driven all the way from France like this, must have been a nightmare. The car was fully loaded, and I MEAN fully loaded, which had the effect of displacing the already low fluid in the reservoir, causing the height control to be ineffective. It just needed a fluid top up, and the car raised to it's normal height. Mr Ferguson was flabergasted when I pointed out the two spare fluid containers in beside the cars toolkit. If only he had phoned me from France, could have saved them a very uncomfortable return trip.

I first had dealings with a certain other customer in the Murray days, when he had a Turbo R and an Aston Martin Virage Volante, although I had never met him until he purchased two cars from Park's, one in 1999, and the other in 2002.
In 1999 he became the proud owner of a bright yellow Bentley Azure, wide bodied Mulliner, with an uprated engine which he had made to his specification. In 2002 he bought a Bentley Arnage extended wheelbase, again built to his specification. At the times, his two cars were believed to be the most expensive in Scotland. Both cars proved to be a headache for both myself and Bentley Motors.

The Azure developed corrosion issues, and had to be repainted several times, not a good advertisement. The Arange, however, gave few problems, but the main concern was the drivers seat. When the owner had visited the factory to spec his car, he sat in a similar car, but could not get comfortable (he was a big man). Bentley in their wisdom, promised that they would tailor a seat to fit him….bad decision. He duly had his new car delivered to his house (payment for it was another story). Surprise surprise, he could not get comfortable. Bentley flew up a chap called Trevor Gaye, who was in charge of the Mulliner division of Bentley.
I took Trevor to the owners factory, where measurements were taken, and Trevor returned to Crewe, A new seat cushion was designed and made, then sent up to myself.

We collected the car and replaced the seat cushion, which unfortunately was not a great deal improved. The owner contacted me again, and said the only way he could get comfortable was to tuck his *"bunnet" under his right thigh when driving.

*For those South of the border in Englandshire, a "bunnet" would be a "flat cap".

My good friend and VIP manager at Bentley, *Tim Hodgson came up with one of the lads from the trim shop, and together, once more to Prestwick to meet our man. He showed us exactly where the "bunnet" needed to be placed to ensure his comfort. Tim returned to the factory and another seat cushion was fabricated and sent up to me. It was an odd looking seat cushion, some 4 inches longer, and steeply padded at the sides, but here's hoping. You know the story by now, car collected, seat fitted and returned – success! Customer was happy. This was reported back to Crewe, and another cushion was made and duly fitted to the passenger seat so they both matched.

This owner always trusted us to do what was needed for his cars, and we had a good relationship, indeed I was invited to his new baby daughters christening. One day, while speaking to him, I asked if he was still off the cigarettes, "nope, back on them" was the reply. This was to have a bearing later on. We had the Arnage in for service, and it was noted that the rear cigar lighter kept blowing fuses. It was burnt out and needed a new unit. I took it upon myself to replace it at £125, and thought all was well. They were always good payers, until there appeared on the scene a new accountant. The invoice was overdue, and when I spoke to the accountant, the only way they would pay the invoice was if I deducted the cost of the cigar lighter which was never authorised. I explained the previous conversation with the owner, and held my ground, saying full payment was due. They sent a cheque minus the £125. Things were never quite the same after that, heaven only knows what that accountant had been saying to him!

*Tim had started his working career with Rolls-Royce as an apprentice in the trim shop and worked his way up to VIP manager. Tim has now retired, but is available as an after dinner speaker. One of the old school, good guy and a great friend.

We had a Range Rover customer turned up one Friday afternoon at 3.30, having been booked for an MOT at 9.00am that morning. He was down for a loan car, which Scott, my service advisor at the time duly arranged. Scott then came to me saying the customer was going to keep the loan car overnight. Now, I knew this customer, and overnight would turn into the weekend and beyond, so I approached the customer who had already loaded his golf cart into my car.

I told him it wasn't possible to keep the car overnight, but we could do his MOT while he waited, would take an hour. He refused, and became very abusive, saying he had to be at the airport. I said, in that case, there's your car back, we are no longer able to help you. He got right in my face but I stood my ground.

Eventually, he took his golf cart and threw it into his Range Rover, at which point it whacked off the rear bumper and hit him in the leg. I tried so hard to keep a straight face!

After a few minutes, he sheepishly came to me and asked if we could still do the MOT while he waited? No problem I replied. The MOT was carried out, and Scott my adviser came to me to tell me it passed okay. I said, right Scott, go and ask him if he has time for us to clean his car. Scott said "but he was to be at the airport". Humour me, I said, lets call his bluff. Scott went into the customer lounge, and spoke to the customer. Yes please, he said, that would be great. So much for the airport.

I retrieved the CCTV footage of the incident with the golf cart, and sent it to my friend Jan at our Ayr Land Rover Branch. This customer a few weeks previously had Jan in tears with his aggression, and when her aftersales manager telephoned the customer asking him not to speak to his staff like that, he got the response that "she is too fucking sensitive!"

This customer several years later, got his face slashed while sitting at the traffic lights in his Bentley, and I believe is now in prison for various crimes. Guess I'm lucky I'm still here, although he did shake hands with me, and I and my team had nothing but respect from him in any subsequent interactions.

Lets just call this customer "Evan". He was not a very nice man, bought a new Arnage from us a good few years ago, and our trainee sales guy had made a mistake in saying the remote control worked the radio, when it only worked the satellite navigation. This was an easy mistake to make, as the remote had a switch saying "Sat Nav/Radio, which I really blame Bentley for, as this should have been modified before any cars were issued. Evan went off his head at delivery, and called the trainee several names, and demanded the remote would be made to work the radio, which was not possible. The trainee offered to pay for a full new system out his own pocket, at which point I stepped in.

Long story short (too late!), that wasn't going to happen, but I agreed the customer would get some matching leather from the factory, which would allow him to make two cushions for the rear seat.
(Did I mention "Evan" owned an upholstery business?)
Now, this is where Karma steps in, several years later. Evan had arranged a test drive overnight in our Continental GT demonstrator. He came in, left his Arnage with us on the Friday night, and set off with our car, accompanied by a woman who was not his wife!
On the Saturday, he called our GM, Gavin, and asked if he could keep the car another night, to which Gavin reluctantly agreed.

Come Sunday, no sign of Evan or our car. Gavin called him, and was told he couldn't bring the car in as he'd been drinking. Gavin said the car must be returned first thing Monday morning, or it would be reported stolen. Come Monday morning, Gavin called one of our friendly traffic cops, and asked him to look out for our demonstrator coming along Bothwell Road, and he did one better than that by pulling in Evan, and giving him the breathalyser, which turned out to be positive!

We got our car back, and Evan was taken to the police station, and subsequently charged. When we opened the boot of our car, we found a Liverpool hotel receipt for their dirty weekend. Evan got his Arnage back a few days later, and I've no idea what happened to him, his car or his marriage. We never saw him again!

Dr Stuart McAlpine first came to me when I had RRS. He had a beautiful two tone Bentley T1 which I looked after for him. He sold that, and bought a Rolls-Royce Shadow 2, registration 1GGE which I continued to look after. When I started with Murrays, he followed me, and went on to buy a lovely Corniche 2 (NUS834) from us in Charing Cross. This was in addition to his Shadow 2, his reasoning was that he had two sons, so that would be one car each when he passed away. Stuart always gave me a bottle at Christmas, and also an envelope with some money for Ian, the technician that always worked on his cars. When I retired, Stuart gave we a lovely card, along with a cheque...a true gentleman. We exchange Christmas cards, and I still keep in touch to see how he is getting on. He had to give up the golf, but still keeps busy, and was caring for his wife Joan, until she passed away. Joan was a lovely lady, they had been married for 67 years. He's still a member of the *RREC

*Rolls-Royce Enthusiasts Club of which I'm also a member, at time of writing I have just been presented with my 20 year lapel badge.

I first met Jim and Linda Orr when they bought their Bentley GT from us. After it's 6 week service, Jim phoned me up to complain there was a mark on his leather dash top, which he thought was us that had damaged it. Armed with suitable cleaners and leather treatments, I jumped in my car and headed to their house in Ayrshire. I looked at the mark which actually turned out to be a very small imperfection in the leather. Now, leather is a natural product, and some irregularities may be expected, even in a Bentley. I offered to replace the dash under warranty, which Jim declined, as he was more than happy with my explanation.

Jim and Linda became my firm friends, and even attended my wedding, such was the rapport we had. Jim was a retired vet, and kept chickens. Anytime he brought his car in, he would bring me some fresh eggs, the like I've never tasted. Being a vet, he knew precisely the correct diet to give the chickens, which paid dividends in the taste of the eggs. One time he came in....no eggs. No eggs Jim I asked? Saddened, he replied, the foxes got them. Although saddened as they were more his pets, he said the foxes must have been hungry, it's only nature.

We still keep in touch, and once this Covid pandemic is over, we'll be heading down to Ayrshire for a visit!

This chapter would not be the same without mentioning Rae Grieve, but as he features in the car sales chapter, I'll leave it there.

Boyd Tunnock, of Tunnocks Caramel Wafer fame had a Rolls-Royce Silver Seraph which at the time was getting a bit tired. We didn't have anything to offer him, as he was always a Rolls-Royce man, and we were only Bentley now. We even tried to fit a Rolls-Royce grille to an Arnage, but due to the curvature of the Bentley front end, that would not be an option. He is now in a Goodwood BMW Rolls-Royce, but I wanted to mention the incident with his Seraph.

He was at a car show, and Boyds driver, John Bain, had a "little" misshap. He ran the Seraph into the back of a RR Corniche, much to the annoyance of it's owner. John swore blind that the Seraph had jumped into gear by itself. The Corniche owner went berserk, thumping his walking stick on the ground in anger, and calling John all the names under the sun.
This car is going to Jack Barclays London to get fixed, and you will be paying for it, at which point Boyd told him to calm down and he will cover the cost. There was very little damage to the Seraph.

John Bain came to me and explained what had happened. I've known John for years, and if he said the car jumped into gear, then that's what happened. I sat in the car, column gear selector in neutral, engine ticking over. I nudged the steering wheel slightly, and the car jumped into drive. Turns out to be a fault with the gear selector. I went down to the Tunnocks factory along with John, and confirmed to Boyd that the car was indeed faulty. This was a relief to both of them, but in particular John, who had been punishing himself since the incident.

I had said to Boyd just to let his insurance take care of the Corniche, but no, he had given his word, and that was that even though the estimate was £52,000! Yes, £52,000, to be paid before repairs would commence. I could understand that, as the Corniche was only worth in the region of £25,000 to £30,000. I called my colleague Stan Christofi who at that time was in charge of the aftersales side of Jack Barclays, and managed to get £12,000 knocked of the bill.
I was in Mitchells restaurant one night on a date, and Boyd was there along with Jim Hamilton (RIP) of Hamiltons dairies, another customer of mine. I had a bit of a blether with them, then had dinner. When I went to pay, Boyd had already taken care of it. A true gentleman, I wrote him a letter thanking him…

In the showroom, at the service desk were two extremely expensive leather chairs for the customers to sit on while discussing their requirements. Now, the chairs were on castors, which on a polished tiled floor was a recipe for disaster! This came one day as a very obese customer tried to sit down. This guy must have weighed in excess of 25 stone, and to say he was "broad across the beam" was an understatement. He was somewhat wider than the arms of the chair, and when he went to sit down, the chair shot backwards into a new GT door, and the customer fell flat on his back, his head thudding against the floor. Now, first instinct was to check the GT door for damage, but I thought it more prudent to check if the customer was ok.

As I was first aid trained, I should have made him comfortable on the floor, after checking him for any injuries. This training flew out the window, and with my adrenaline in full flow, I howked all 25 plus stone of him back onto his feet! I assisted him over to the customer lounge, where I sat him down and gave him a cup of tea. After a few minutes, he was fine, and so was the Bentley the chair had collided with. No further action was called for, but I did make an entry in the accident book, just in case he decided to sue us, which never happened.

Ian Grant Purdie was a gentleman, I'd known him since the Appleyard days, and I believe he was the man that introduced photocopiers to Scotland many moons ago.

Any time a new model Rolls-Royce or Bentley was introduced, he would have it. I was only really involved with him in the latter years, and big John Finlay and Fraser Anderson would be his contacts. Grant (as he preferred to be called) lived in a penthouse on the Great Western Road in Glasgow, and his garage was never meant for a car the size of a Bentley, indeed it was almost a standing joke when he bought a new car, that a slot would be booked in or bodyshop to fix the damage to the nearside wing he would invariably hit off the garage door!

I have a letter from Grant, when he had issues with his 3 week old Arnage T. He called me from his hotel in Strasbourg, France, after the hotel receptionist had phoned him to tell him "Mr Purdie, your car is calling for you". The alarm was going off, so I reassured him the battery would most likely be at fault, but the second battery would make sure the car would still drive without issue.

To cut a long story short, I found out his next stop would be in Rouffach, near the German and Swiss border.

I arranged for an English speaking technician from Bentley Zurich to meet him, equipped with a new battery and whatever else may be needed. Indeed, the dealer principal from Zurich called Mr Purdie to tell him help was on it's way. It was the battery, and was duly replaced, and his holiday was completed without further hiccup. I still have his letter in my portfolio, which I will treasure.

Grants last car I sold him didn't have coachlines, which he wanted, so I fitted them, albeit taped lines, but he was delighted. I was involved with selling his car from his estate when he sadly passed away.

RIP Grant Purdie

I first met a young James Turnbull back in the days of RRS, when he had a red Mercedes SL. He introduced himself, saying charge him plenty, as he was one of the fussiest guys in the world, and if his car wasn't right, we would be getting it back until it was!

Now we had to repair and paint the N/S F wing, and the car being red, there was always a chance that although the car would look fine in the daylight, under the then orange street lamps, the new paint could appear orange! So, we worked late on the car, then once it was dark, checked it under the street lamps. Bang on, colour was perfect, one delighted customer. James has followed me ever since, and we keep in touch to this day, currently he has a RR Phantom, a Bentley Continental GT, and a RR Silver Shadow over and above his day to day cars.

One day a chap came into RRS having been recommended by James. He had a Jaguar XJS and his name was William Alasdair Lindsay, but preferred to be called Alasdair. He had a bad vibration after having just picked up his car from service at another garage. I took me about 5 minutes to diagnose that the front wheels were loose! Tightened them up and checked all was okay. Another customer to add to my customer base. Alasdair progressed with his cars, and eventually had a Rolls-Royce Phantom. He was into property among other things, indeed helping me out with a lovely flat when I was going through my divorce.

Alasdair very sadly passed away in March 2019, at the age of 60. A life taken far too soon.

RIP Alasdair Lindsay 1959 - 2019

There were occasions where an overdue account or bad debt had to be chased up, this wasn't the most pleasant of tasks, but had to be done. Several memorable ones spring to mind.

When myself and Jimmy were still doing homers, we had a Silver Shadow owner who owed us around *£400. Now, he owned a pub called "Rockwells, Drinks for Heroes" at the then fruit market, which is now the Merchant City in Glasgow.

One evening, Jimmy and myself decided we would pay him a visit. We walked into his pub, his Silver Shadow was parked at the door, and armed with a tyre lever each, we found our man sitting drinking at one of the tables, along with some three or four young ladies. There was nobody else in the pub. Billy big boots promptly introduced us "his two mechanics that look after my Rolls-Royce", only to cut himself short when he noticed our tyre levers. "What are the levers for guys?" he enquired. I said they're to take your hubcaps off, and you'll get them back when you pay us what you owe us. At that time, a Shadow hubcap or wheel trim cost around £400.

"You can't do that" he said."Just watch us" I replied. "Hold on, hold on, I can give you half just now, and half later. "Fine" I said, Jimmy, just take two of his hubcaps, and Jimmy headed for the door.

"Wait wait, let me see what I've got in the safe," and I followed him into the office, and promptly collected the full amount.

* This amount was full declared on my annual HMRC tax return officer, honest!

In the days of RRS, when I was on my own working out of the garage in Maryhill, I had a customer, Gerry Lipton, dropped his car off, asking me to fix the brakes on his Silver Shadow, as he had a hydraulic warning light on. He was off on holiday to Spain for two weeks, so I just had to do what was needed. Turned out it needed an accumulator and valve body overhaul, and as this was in the days before mobile phones, I couldn't get hold of him, so carried on and repaired it. I knew (or so I thought) that he would pay me when he got back, so I delivered the car ready for his return.

A good few attempts to get him on the phone, culminated in his response "I didn't authorise this, I assumed it was just a bulb or something!" so I'm not paying.

I went down to his office in Eglington Toll, and went in to see him. He was sitting at his desk, and asked me why I had brought tools with me. I told him in no uncertain terms that as he had not paid, the parts fitted were still mine, and I am going to take them back off his car.

"You can't do that" he retorted. "Watch me!", and went towards his car. All of a sudden, the money appeared, and I was paid in full. Gerry Lipton passed away many years ago, and his business sold on.

Again, in the RRS days, only this time in Hillington, I had a customer called Ian, who I knew fairly well, had his Mercedes 380SL recovered into us, the prognosis not great. Next step was to remove the engine, and strip for assessment, which Ian duly asked us to do.

The engine was scrap, having thrown a connecting rod through the side of the cylinder block. A new engine, cost wise was totally out of the question, so I tried to source a second hand unit to no avail.

Ian decided he would just take the car back to his own garage, and wait until either an engine could be found, or he could afford a new one.

I let him trailer the car away, but I retained all the engine ancillary parts, ie the radiator, coolers, air conditioning etc etc., and gave him his bill for what we had done so far.

Some time later, he came in looking for his remaining parts, as he has sold the car the way it was. I said fine, just settle the bill, and you can take them. "I'm paying nothing! You didn't fix the car so I don't owe you anything!"

I took the bill off him, ripped it up, grabbed him by the scruff of his neck and seat of his pants, and frog marched him the full length of the workshop, and threw him out the back door.

I told him I would be selling his parts to recover my money, and told him never to return. A week or so later, he sheepishly returned, and apologised, and offered a cheque in payment. "You must be joking" I said, "it needs to be cash!". He went away and returned with the cash, and duly collected all the parts. Believe it or not, we became friends after all that, but have lost touch with him, as he has moved away.

The previous three examples would never have been allowed legally or otherwise, if it hadn't been for the fact I had nobody to report to, the buck stopped with me.

The following is an example of when I was with Bentley Glasgow, under Douglas Park. A customer owed us around £300, and several phone calls brought no results. On the last call, he said he was going to phone "Dougie" Park, as he was a friend of his, and explain why he hadn't paid. I suggested that would be a mistake, but he was insistent. About two minutes later, I got a call from Douglas Park, telling me to go round to the guys fucking house, and sit on his fucking doorstep until he paid up! Anyone who is a real friend of Douglas wouldn't dream of calling him "Dougie"!
I got in my car and went round to the debtors house, where his wife asked me in and gave me a cup of tea while I waited. Our man duly arrived, and I told him I wasn't leaving until I got paid. I got paid!

I first met Billy Tennant in the RRS days, when he had a Silver Spirit. Billy had followed me right up to the time I left the trade (and beyond). Billy is an avid petrol head, always having something interesting in his garage. Currently has a Bentley GT, and several other cars and motorbikes. Billy has been most helpful to me when I was upgrading the house, and him and his good lady, Lynne were at my wedding. We often have an afternoon at my house, playing pool and setting the world to rights.

I always tried to treat customers with respect, and also to treat them the way they would expect to be treated. I had a customer, a successful businessman, who owned a Rolls-Royce and a Bentley at the time. We had inspected the car for an alleged brake fault, but could not find anything amiss. I took the car back after extensive testing, and spoke to the owner. He said there was definitely a brake failure, so I asked if he could give me any further information, eg, were there any warning lights on, to assist with any repairs needed. He said " that's your job, now run along son, just get it fixed!" That last remark cost him several thousands of pounds, as we renewed virtually the full braking system! Respect works both ways…

During the Bentley Glasgow time, our parts department sold a set of wheels to an Asian gentleman, who sent his father in to collect them. Turns out the card was stolen, and we got a severe bollocking from head office about taking card payments over the phone.

I tried to see what the registration number of the van that collected the wheels was on our CCTV, but it was such poor quality, the registration number could not be made out. Worse than useless, what chance did we have. Never did get the money back.

Being forewarned and wary, we had another chap buy two suspension struts, and sent them to a house address by courier. What could go wrong. They were delivered to, as I found out later, to a high rise flat, and again the card was fraudulent. I sat outside that house for ages, hoping the guy would reappear, which of course he didn't. It was in a less desirable area of Glasgow, not a decent car in sight.

Another bollocking from head office, never got the money back, and the money deducted from my accounts. No bonus that month then. At the time of my retirement, the police had arrested the guy in Liverpool, and were still conducting their investigation.

Chapter Eleven – The tricky jobs

When I was with Appleyards, we had a customer with a Silver Shadow 2, who had an issue with the windscreen wipers while still under warranty. The owner lived from memory around the Carlisle area, and was not prepared to put the miles on the car to bring it to us.

Myself and our electrician, Gordon Adam were instructed to take our new *Shadow 2 demonstrator, tools and everything we might need to repair the car. Obviously we did not know at this point what was required, so we were told to swop anything we needed from the demonstrator.

We drove to the customers house, and checked out his car. It was an issue with the drivers side wiper wheelbox, which involved stripping the dash to get access, a pig of a job, particularly having to do it on both cars. We got there in the end, although it took a good few hours. A happy customer though, which was the main thing.

*Our demonstrator was affectionately known as "402", due to its private registration number, G402.

Still with Appleyard, there was a recall announced on Shadow 2/Bentley T2 gearboxes. It involved draining the fluid, removing the sump, and installing another safety switch in the gearbox valve body. I had done quite a few, but some other dealers hadn't done any, and only had a very few applicable vehicles on their database, so it was considered more cost effective to send me to carry out the recalls, the two that stick in my memory was the dealer in Aberdeen, and the one in Carlisle.

Got me out for a while, which was good!

We had a customer who was over 6 feet tall, and when his new Shadow 11 arrived, he could not get the seat down low enough, due to the reduced headroom caused by the factory fitted sunroof, which no one had mentioned to him.

What is to be done? We contacted the factory, and they authorised us to fit Australian seat mountings, which, due to the Australian driver being on average taller than the UK driver (allegedly), were lower. This was not a simple task, the full interior, carpets and soundproofing had to be removed. The old seat mountings were cut and ground off the transmission tunnel and floor, and the new, lower mounts were welded on.

Guess who got the job? Yup, moi! I enjoyed doing it, as it was a bit of a change from the routine. Duly done, all corrosion treatment applied, and everything built back up. It all resulted in a happy customer, which was the main objective. I often wonder if there are any small Australians…..

Moving onto the Gaulds era, which was the introduction of the "SZ" range, basically the Silver Spirit. One of the main changes was the introduction of mineral oil, (similar to Citroen) in place of the RR363 brake fluid as used in the previous models.

This was all fine and dandy until an owner would top the system up with brake fluid instead of mineral oil. This caused a catastrophic contamination of the system, requiring that every brake and suspension component with rubber seals, had to be replaced. Any metal pipes etc, had to be thoroughly cleaned out with methylated spirits, and blown dry with compressed air. A mammoth job, and at the time cost around £5,000 plus to rectify.

Trying to stop this from happening again, the reservoir tops were drilled, wired and sealed with a lead seal, so that only dealers could top up the system. Subsequent models had special reservoir tops that would only accept the correct adaptor on the fluid bottle.

Moving swiftly onto the Douglas Park time, we had a Continental GT not long after they were introduced, which exhibited a missfire and the engine management light was on. *Derek Ferrar (AKA - Deek), my master technician was allocated the job. He traced the fault to coolant being pumped up the engine wiring harness, from one of the electric coolant pumps, and contaminating the Electronic Control Unit (ECU) for the engine management. One of the electric coolant pump seals had failed, causing the issue. Worse was yet to come, as coolant had found it's way into the cars main wiring loom.

The factory wanted the car back, and they would fit a new wiring loom, as no one had ever attempted this before. Deek was having none of it! He wanted to carry out the repair, and given his experience and work ethic, it was authorised. It would be a major task, the car was stripped, engine, transmission, suspension, full interior, front wings, basically the car was a rolling shell.

I had started Derek as an apprentice when he was 16, and he has stayed loyal to me ever since...one of the good guys.

The wiring loom arrived, weighing in at some 75kg, and in a box half the size of a Ford Fiesta!

The factory sent an engineer up in the latter stages, purely to see how it was done, as there was another car with the same issue in Australia!

In the meantime, the owner was without his Bentley, and the factory were not in a position to loan him another one, although they authorised a 7 Series BMW. Now, the customer was a very wealthy individual, who owned several cars, one of which was a 7 Series BMW, so this was now a matter of principal. I spoke to my friend Tim Hodgson at Crewe with the suggestion we recompense the owner with a monitory gesture, of £5,000, which would be roughly the same amount if Bentley were to hire a BMW for him for the length of time the Bentley was in the workshop. I spoke to the customer, saying why don't we get you a cheque for that amount, and you can take your good lady on a holiday while we fix your car. He readily agreed, and everyones face was saved.

The repairs were completed, and the car rebuilt. I have to say, it started first time, and I tested the car with Deek, and there was not a squeak or rattle from anywhere, which was amazing, given the severity and amount of stripping that was done. The car ran faultlessly, was fully valeted, filled with fuel and returned to the owner.

When Deeks hours were added up, he had spent some 186 hours on the job, the cost of which was settled by Bentley at our hourly rate, with no questions asked. The Bentley area aftersales manager brought Deek a Bentley jacket as a small token of their appreciation. Good result all round.

We had a Turbo R in for service, and the customer mentioned the alloy wheels were corroded, other than replacing the wheels, was there anything we could do?

Now, this was a good few years ago, long before the many wheel repair centres that are currently in existence, so I made the decision to have the wheels powder coated by a small firm in Larkhall. The wheels looked great and the customer was delighted, that is until a few weeks later, the drivers front wheel broke in two on the motorway at 70mph! Fortunately, the owners chauffeur was an ex police driver, and didn't panic, instead bringing the car to a halt in a fairly controlled manner.

We recovered the car in, and found the remaining three wheels were all cracked. Customer was obviously not happy to say the least, but I promised him I would get an answer. In the meantime, he insisted, and rightly so, we replace all the wheels, including the spare which hadn't been touched. I didn't argue, as he had us over a barrel.

I spoke to Bentley technical at the factory, and they agreed to carry out a full metallurgical test on the broken wheel. It turned out that the wheel had been weakened by over 75%, most likely due to being heated up to over 180 degrees during the powder coating process. Of course the guy that did them denied it, and as a small business, we decided not to pursue things through the courts, as it would bring attention to us, and it would probably be a waste of time anyway.

I had appeased the customer, who, although he could have, didn't take it any further… Phew!

During service, or on customer complaint of a pump noise from the N/S/F of GT or Spur, a vacuum leak was identified. The first one we did a smoke test on the vacuum pipe, which was down to me as I smoked at the time, and blew fag smoke up the pipe and watched for where it came out, thus identifying where the leak was. Highly technical! Subsequently, we had access to a proper smoke tester, as I'd given up smoking!

Now, this particular leaking pipe required removal of the engine to even see it. Good design! It was okay, sort of, if the car had a warranty, hard lines for the owner if not. The pipe itself was £170, but the rest of the not unsubstantial bill was made up of labour and various bolts etc, which were "one use" only.

They later changed the design of the pipe, as the leaks were caused by a split at the plastic pipe, just at the "T" piece, which was metal. The two different rates of expansion eventually caused the split. Later pipes were all plastic, which they should have been in the first place due to the extremely high levels of heat in these W12 engine bays.

We had another GT, out of warranty and brought into us on a transporter. The engine was "knocking it's head off", and on speaking to the factory, it was deemed to require a new engine. At that time, other than minor repairs, no stripping of the W12 engine was authorised.
A new engine was ordered, but was it fair that such a car should need a new engine? Most certainly not, and on discussing with our factory area manager, it was decided to provide the new engine free of charge, the customer paying for the not inconsiderable labour. I pursued this further, and eventually the factory agreed to foot the entire bill. As they should. Customer was delighted, and I still have his personal letter to me, hand written. For one of Scotlands wealthiest men to take the time to do that means a lot...the customer? None other than Sir Tom Hunter….
I still have the letter, one to treasure.

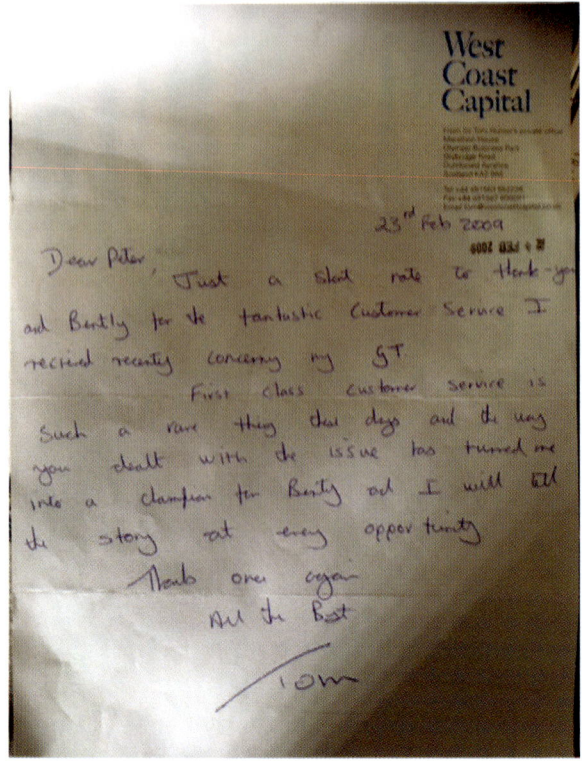

Regarding the rule not to strip the W12, we had another GT in with a noisy tappet. The factory told us it would require a new engine, until I informed them the car was still under warranty. All of a sudden, a new hydraulic tappet was sent up, costing from memory eleven or twelve quid, and this was fitted in less than an hour. Shortly thereafter, the "no strip" rule was relaxed, but only slightly. Common sense had prevailed for once!

As you can imagine, rattles on any car are most annoying, but on a Bentley even more so. We had one owner, Brian McGuigan, who had a rattle from the front of his Continental Flying Spur. We suspected the front brake calipers, but was difficult to find the sort of road surface which we could reproduce the noise. Eventually, up the back of Hamilton, we found a suitable stretch of road. We named this road "McGuigan Street" after the owner!
This was to be our test route for any further customer issues with rattles, until we went up there one day, and the buggers had resurfaced the road! The search was on again for a new "McGuigan Street"!

Bentley in their wisdom, decided to change the front subframe mountings from rubber to metal on the Continental GT, which was to make the steering and suspension more taut, therefore more of a drivers car. There had to be a sacrifice however, in the noise level at low speed over certain undulating road surfaces.
If a customer complained, new "modified" front dampers were to be fitted. This made no difference whatsoever.

We had a customer from Aberdeen, and although he didn't buy the car from us, as always, I was more than happy to look after it for him. He would not accept this noise level was normal, indeed his car was noisier than some others. We went through the routine of replacing the dampers, with no effect. The car was returned to the unhappy customer until a further plan could be organised.
I knew what the issue was, but Bentley would not allow us to replace the subframe with the earlier type, as the car had been *homologated for the metal type.

*Homologation is the process to certify a vehicle or components in a vehicle that satisfies the requirements set by various statutory regulatory bodies.

We had to do something, the customer was on the point of rejecting the car, not to us, but to his supplying dealer. Not a situation anyone would relish.

I hatched an unofficial plan, along with our factory area manager, Jonathan Morris. We would order up two subframes, one of the new type, and one with the older rubber type. We got the car back in, and replaced the subframe with the correct type. If anything, the noise was no better, indeed it was worse. We then replaced the subframe with the rubber mounted type, perfect, noise gone! Bentley would not permit us to leave it there, we had to refit the cars original subframe and return the car to the owner, while a decision was made on the way forward.

The owner was fine with this, as he knew I was on the case, and also he was out of the country for weeks on end, so lack of use wasn't an issue. He just wanted his car right.

Bentley had to carry out this alteration to one of their own cars, and fully test and evaluate the modification, as it could affect steering, handling, ABS, and any other connected systems. Load of pish in my mind, but necessary I suppose.

Many weeks later, I got a phone call on my mobile, about 7:30 on a Friday night, to give me the unofficial heads up that our solution had been approved. It was made official on the Monday, and I contacted the owner. We collected the car once more, and fitted the new subframe. The owner was delighted, and said so in a very complimentary email, which I wish I had kept.

When I was later in Amalfi on the Elite club trip, Steve O'Hara, member of the board at Bentley, thanked me and the team for all the good work we had put into this. We did get paid in full under warranty for all the hours we had put in.

An owner traded in his Spur for a later model. The new car exhibited a "heartbeat" noise on tickover, all air con, radio etc. had to be switched off to hear this noise. I checked several other similar cars, and they too had this "heartbeat" when they warmed up. I demonstrated this to the customer, who seemed to accept it, although not happy that his new car was noisier than the old one. I could understand his concerns, but not one other owner ever heard this noise. Not many people switch their air con and radio off to listen for noises!

Now, this is where Bentley made a rod for their own back. I reckoned, if anything, it was a harmonic noise from the engine, which had been altered from the previous one. Bentley wanted us to change the gearbox crossmember, and put a special damper on the propeller shaft bearing. These modifications made no difference. They then instructed is, after various attempts at moving the flywheel to torque convertor relationship, to finally replace the gearbox. Engine out to do that, and made no difference whatsoever.

Bentley motors then decided they wanted the car back to Crewe, where they replaced the engine. I got the car back one Saturday morning, hastily finished on the Friday night, as the guy who was working on it was going on holiday. The car wasn't clean, and there were several dents on the front wings due to persons or persons unknown leaning on them with their elbows. The noise, however was away! Apart from the new engine, I never did find out what the cause was. Maybe they fitted a "new, old type" engine? I don't know, only my opinion, but how much did that whole escapade cost them, where it could have been avoided by sticking to their guns, as it was a characteristic of the car.

I'm all for keeping a customer happy, and fortunately we never had anyone else pick up the noise. I found myself checking every Flying Spur when they came in for service or whatever, and they all had this "heartbeat".

We sold a Bentayga to a lovely gentleman called Henry Souttar, from Kings Lynn. He bought it from us on a recommendation from a friend who we had previously sold a motorcar to.

The issue started 172 miles from Bentley Glasgow, on his way home with his new motor car. He and his good lady stopped at a motorway service station, and smelled burning from the car. They thought at first it must be a lorry or something, couldn't be their new Bentley...or could it? On further investigation, there was oil leaking onto the exhaust. There followed a catalogue of catastrophes, which was most certainly not a good advert for Bentley.

The recovery truck didn't arrive until after eight o'clock, with the Souttars waiting at the service station. The car was eventually loaded up, with instructions to bring back to us, rather than the nearest dealer which would have been Bentley Leeds.

A taxi was arranged to take Mr And Mrs Souttar to Leeds airport, where a hire car was waiting.

After a hair raising manic taxi ride, they were dropped off at the wrong side of the airport for the hire car. They got an airport bus and eventually reached the hire operation. They were shown to their car, a small basic Toyota "puddle jumper" with no sat nav, but as they are both retired, in a strange place, they just wanted to get home after a horrendous first experience.

The following day, still no sign of their Bentley getting dropped off to us. No one seemed to know where the car was, turned out it was in a storage depot, and we didn't get it until the following day.

Eventually, it got dropped off, and Steven Goldie (Stevie the beard) was given the job. The oil was leaking between the engine and the gearbox, so an endoscope was used to investigate. Not conclusive as there was too much oil around. Bentley called in an expert from the gearbox manufacturer, who wanted us to replace the transmission as a precaution.

At this point, the customer was rejecting the car, and who could blame him. Before he retired, Henry Souttar owned a successful garage, and he himself was an engineer to trade. I thought he would be interested in what the fault was, so perhaps not something I would do for many customers, but I sent him photos and videos of the engine and transmission removal. This had a positive effect, as he could see how professional we were in our undertaking of the repair.

Once the units were removed, and the gearbox parted from the engine, we could see a split rubber seal at the rear of the engine. This has obviously been nicked on assembly at the factory, and taken almost 200 miles to start leaking. Over the many phone calls with Henry, I built up a great rapport, he was such an interesting character, and as one engineer to another, he agreed with me that he would take the car back!

By this time, the loan puddle jumper had been replaced with an S Class Mercedes, so the plan was hatched. Mr and Mrs Souttar would drive to the Factory in Crewe, where they would be given a VIP tour, then taken to the 5 star Rookery hotel, where they would spend the night. They would then be collected after breakfast and taken to Crewe station, where they would get a train to Glasgow.

Minor hiccup in that our service advisor was asked to book the Rookery, which she did, but unknown to us, there are two Rookery hotels, and the one in London was booked. This was sorted out and paid for before any further disasters struck.

We collected them in a chauffeur driven Bentley Mulsanne, and took them to the Crossbasket Castle Hotel where they would dine and spend the night with our compliments. After breakfast, we collected them and brought to the dealership.

I gave them the VIP tour of the dealership, including McLaren, and introduced them to our staff, in particular *Stevie the Beard, who had successfully carried out the repairs. Stevie echoed my words to Henry, that is "I don't care how long you take, just make the car right"

*** Stevie the Beard was so named because he had a rather large red beard... now there's a surprise!*

They spent almost the full day at the dealership, before returning home in their Bentley for the second time, after another full handover.

I had retired by the time their first annual service was due, but I found out they were coming in, so I went in to say hello. They were such a lovely couple, and had stayed in the Crossbasket Castle again, after driving all the way from Kings Lynn. I don't know if they still come all the way for service, I doubt it, as I see their friend who recommended them has bought another car, but not from Bentley Glasgow. Maybe because of this Covid Pandemic? Who knows.....

Another Bentayga tale, this one resulted in a buy back. The owner had complained of several intermittent electrical issues, generally around the door and tailgate locking and operation. We could never fault the car at the time of testing, the factory even sent up two of their technicians, who could not fault the car, but changed over many units as a precaution. Customer took the car back, but subsequently said all the faults were still present, albeit still intermittently.

I used the car personally for a full week, and couldn't get the car to misbehave. Eventually, it was decided to take the car back and give him a new one. Guess what, the new car was just the same!

Between us, we worked out what eventually was the issue. Nothing wrong with the car, it was a characteristic on the engine stop/start system. If the car was brought to a halt, and the engine stopped itself, meant that the car wasn't fully switched off, causing the doors not to unlock, and the tailgate to require two presses to open. If the car was brought to a halt, and manually switched off, the doors and tailgate were fine. Red faces all round between the owner, ourselves, and most of all Bentley, who were not aware this would happen.

We bought in a Rolls-Royce Phantom (Goodwood Phantom) from a customer who had hit hard times. Only issue with the car was that the owner had his wife's name inlaid in the veneer on the Glove box panel. Obviously seemed a good idea at the time, but unless we found a new owner with the same name, it had to go. The parts were costed at over £2500 from the dealer in Edinburgh, as the full dash veneer would have to be replaced to ensure a match. I called Chapman and Cliff, who have carried out various woodwork restorations in the past for me. They said send the panel to them and they would do what they could. A week later and a bill for £90 (yes, Ninety pounds!) and the panel arrived back with us, a perfect match. Boy, they are good….

McLaren would give their share of problems, but none more so than with battery issues, mainly due to the car not getting used. Once the car was started, if left ticking over, it could cut out due to low voltage. This had the adverse effect of causing the door deadlock not to release, stranding the driver in a locked car. This happened once to Rory, our valeter who started to panic. We came to his rescue, but only after the emergency boot release was used, which was under a front wheel arch, then a battery pack used to power up the door locks.

This happened with a customer, fortunately he saw the funny side of it. Trapped in the car, he phoned McLaren assistance who came to his rescue, albeit after a few hours. He joked with us that it wouldn't have been so bad, but he was bursting for a pee! Think I would have smashed a window and got out!

We had a McLaren P1 in for warning light issues, which turned out to be a faulty battery. Not the little 12 volt battery, but the main hybrid battery, costing some £68,000 pounds!

The car was out of warranty, so the owner was faced with a bill for some £78,000 including the labour and VAT.

I approached Paul Saunders, our McLaren area manager, and it was agreed that McLaren would pay for the battery, owner to pay the labour. Subsequently, McLaren agreed to foot the whole bill. The battery arrived, but it was a reconditioned unit, fair enough, but then Derek, my technician came to me, unable to fit the battery, as they had not replaced the coolant hoses which were cracked.

Just to put a picture in your mind, the battery was about the width of the car, and major stripping was required for access. The battery is also cooled from the vehicle cooling system. We were not allowed to touch the battery as it was some 600 volts, and only authorised personnel were permitted. Another call later, and a lad from the battery manufacturers came and replaced the hoses. Job done, happy customer.

I have encountered many difficult issues in my years in the trade, we always got there in the end though, I always had a great team behind me, ain't no mountain high enough!

Chapter Twelve – High Jinks, Monkey business and Shenanigans.

Some of the escapades we got up to would not go down well in todays motor trade...health and safety? Never heard of it!
Several instances spring to mind.......

In the days when you cleaned and tested spark plugs rather than just replace them, we had a machine that sand blasted the plugs clean, but also sent some 12,000+ volts through it to check the performance. Now, 12,000 volts may seem a lot, and it is, but the amperage wasn't very high, so although you got a right jolt, it wasn't fatal (thankfully). Any one of you who has experienced a shock from the high tension (HT) leads of a car will know what I'm talking about.
Now, here's the fun bit... we would hook the wire to the nearby bench vice, and ask one of the younger apprentices to clamp something in the vice. When they were touching the vice, the button was pressed, sending, you guessed it, 12,000 volts through the vice and them. How we laughed! They soon became wise to this, and looked for the wire anytime they went to the vice. I thought, right, something better is called for, so I went under the bench, connecting the wire to the vice so the wire wasn't seen, and then one of my colleagues, Big John Graham, saw what I was doing and pressed the button...you guessed it again, 12,000 volts, but through me this time. With the shock, I jumped up (under the bench) and whacked my head off the underside...talk about Karma.......

Big John Graham had a signature trick, that whenever he was replacing a set of exhaust manifold gaskets, while the manifold was off, he would put a couple of handfuls of grease in the exhaust. As soon as the car was started, the hot exhaust turned the grease into smoke, which in turn filled the workshop. What the fuck's going on here, big Findlay would erupt! Just the grease I used to seat the new gaskets, Big Graham would reply! Guess he thought big Findlay came up the Clyde on a banana boat....
Regularly, if one of the younger apprentices gave up cheek, he would be locked in the boot of a Silver Shadow, then driven up and down the workshop....this was well and good, until one day, about 5.30pm, I was

clocking out, and I was aware of muffled shouts coming from the direction of a Silver Shadow. Oops, an apprentice had been in there since tea break at 3.00pm – sorry Barry!

Another punishment for cheeky apprentices was to grab them, hold their back against the side of a Silver Shadow, and jam their wrists in the electric windows...wasn't enough to cause pain (I think) but just enough so they couldn't escape. The car was then driven up and down the workshop, just at a speed where the apprentice could march sideways at the same rate. All these things were generally carried out when big Findlay was out for his lunch!

Some lunchtimes, if the weather was okay, we would go out the back to the football pitch, and have a game. Someone brought in an old Honda 90 moped type thing, and we got it going. This was my first ever go on a motorbike, not very successfully, as somehow I managed to pull a wheelie, and I slid off the back, but still holding on to the handlebars, and consequently the throttle was held wide open. (I have subsequently found out that this is known as a"Whisky throttle" for some unknown reason!) I seem to remember it went for ages over the bumpy ground, with my nether regions banging up and down against the luggage rack. My only way of stopping was to fall off! Fortunately didn't break anything on either myself or the bike! This didn't dissuade me from wanting a motor bike!

Mike, one of the mechanics (not to be confused with the pop group Mike and the Mechanics) suggested that all the other mechanics chip in a fiver, and they could be joint owners of a petrol engined, radio control model of a motor torpedo boat (MTB) that he would build. The apprentices weren't allowed to chip in, nor could we afford to, as that would have been a weeks wages! The plan was that once Mike had built it, lunchtimes would be spent across the road at Maxwell Park pond….that was the theory anyway. We had a concrete trough in the workshop, where we washed our hands, and this was to be the "running-in" test bed for the newly completed boat. For the next week or so, we were subjected to the racket of Mike carefully running the engine in ready for the big launch.
So, one nice day at lunchtime, we all trooped over to Maxwell Park pond, and Mike, the skipper, had first shot. The boat was started up, and put in

the water, under the "capable" hands of Mike. All went well for a while, until, maybe it went out of range, but Mike lost control, and the boat headed for the concrete side of the pond at full throttle!

Big John Graham ran like the wind to try and save it, but it hit the bank and flew through the air into a tree. I fear if Big John did catch it the propeller would have ripped his hand off! We (the apprentices) found it so funny, much to the annoyance of all those that had chipped in. I always remember, the little life raft that had fallen off on impact, being the only thing left bobbing up and down in the pond…..

Ian Fraser, one of the directors had a racing Mini Cooper S, which had ended up in our workshop. I was to park it outside, so I got it started. As you will recall from earlier, the whole place was about quarter of a mile long, with the lane running the full length alongside, so I decided to see how quickly this Mini could go!
I had to quickly park it at the top end of the lane, outside the paint shop and hide. I had roared past the directors office, and he ran up the lane to catch whoever was driving. He was raging, but I was never caught – just as well or I no doubt wouldn't be here writing this!

In those days it wasn't so frowned upon to go to the pub at lunchtime on a Friday, and myself and my pal and colleague, Jimmy would go along to Sammy Dows pub in Nithsdale Road for a couple of pints. Often we would be accompanied by John Mulligan ("Spike"), who always made us laugh with his stories, he talked so much that usually we had finished our pints, and he had hardly touched his, only stopping to breathe!
A new pub opened up in 1977 at Crossmyloof just up the road and was called the Jean Armour. Jimmy and myself decided to go there one Friday for a change. This was the first day of opening, so wee stood at the bar, blethering as usual, and two pints later was time to go back to work. Oops, when we turned round, all we could see was oily footprints on the light coloured carpet, leading up to the bar, and all the "shuffle" marks on the carpet where we had been standing with our manky boots. Didn't go back there for a while!
I later got a job in there, on the door at weekends, and occasional bar work.

We used to lock ourselves in at the end of the evening, downing pints, eating crisps and nuts, and playing Space Invaders. This came to an abrupt end when the alarm company noticed we were leaving about 3.30am and informed the owner. The owner of the pub, John Waterson also had a Silver Shadow, which I did homers on.

One day, Gerry Nicol (Nick) and myself were sent to a breakdown on a Morris Marina – not starting. Armed with some tools and jump leads, we set off for an address in Kircaldy Road. Now, remember, this was in the days well before satellite navigation and mobile phones, we headed for Kircaldy, as a couple of know-alls, we new Kircaldy Road was in Kircaldy, or at least heading there! Hmmm, an hour or so later, we could find neither hide nor hair of Kircaldy Road. We headed back to Glasgow, to George Square to be precise, where we knew there was a Glasgow map on the tourist information board situated in the square.
Oops! Kircaldy Road was not, as we thought, near or in Kircaldy, but across the road from the garage! We headed back, just in time to see the guys pushing the Marina across Springkell Avenue into the workshop. Boy, did we get a bollocking from big John!

We took on a new apprentice, Stevie Archibald, later to become a professional footballer, which is just as well, because he couldn't put a nut in a monkeys mouth! (Sorry Stevie). Stevie and I occasionally still keep in contact, at time of writing, he is living in Spain.
Anyway, I digress. Taking Stevie on meant that he inherited the "tea boy" duties (Phewww!)
One day, he had forgotten to get a Mars Bar for one of the mechanics, who shall remain nameless, and was duly sent back to the shop to wait in the queue, much to Stevie's annoyance. He returned with a large smirk on his face, gave the Mars Bar over to the mechanic, and sat down beside me. When the mechanic took a bite of his chocolate bar, Stevie started giggling, and whispered to me that he had secretly opened the Mars wrapper, and having a hole in his trouser pocket, this allowed him to rub the chocolate bar against, well, lets just say his manhood! I then erupted in a fit of giggles too, and to this day none of the others had a clue why. Until now that is!

Big John Findlay, being an avid football fan, allowed Stevie time off every week to go training for Clyde FC, which Stevie ended up leaving us to play for professionally. We were good friends and often hung around together outwith work, tinkering with our cars.

As previously mentioned, the customer service reception was in the workshop, in Big Findlay's office. We had a customer, Mr Monachan, and his wife come in to collect their Rolls-Royce. They had just picked up their two boys from the private school not far from us. From memory, the boys were between about 6 and 8 years old, and into everything in the workshop. Nick one day handed one of them the manky grease gun, and told the other to touch the greasy screw on our ramp. You can imagine the state they were in and got a leathering from their mum! We were knotting ourselves!

One of our jokes we played on new apprentices, was to let them "overhear" our conversations about the "Appleyard Glee Club", and when curiosity got the better of them, we told them or club met every Friday, in the Vintners Pub on the Broomielaw, in Glasgows town centre. This, in retrospect was particularly cruel, as the Vintners was a well know gay bar. We would be greeted with "you bastards!" when the apprentice came back in to work on the Monday morning. Obviously none of us were at the Vintners on the Friday.....or were we?
We would also send new apprentices to the shop for a packet of "Mint Eylashes" or "Everlasting Zoob Zoobs!"

We were paid weekly (very weakly) in those days, cash in a brown envelope with the payslip written on the outside. Every Friday afternoon, a queue would form outside the wages office, and a lovely lady called Myra if memory serves me correctly, handed out the pay packets from her window. One day, I fashioned a, lets just say "gentleman's appendage" out of black "dum-dum" putty, and stick it to the wall underneath her window. She never saw it, but everyone else did! Not childish at all!
I did a similar thing a few years later when in Gaulds, but this time stuck it on the front grille of Bob Martins Austin Allegro – it was a few days before he noticed it...

We had been relocated in Kirklee Road in the West End, and one of our lunchtime pursuits was to troop over to the pond on Great Western Road, and hire some paddle boats. Right bunch of *weans!

*For readers South of the border, "Weans" is a term of endearment meaning children.

One fine day, we were all there, and it was decided to grab one of the apprentices, and swing him over the pond, on the pretence of throwing him in. Oops! We did, and he was soaked to the skin. He had to go home and get a change of clothes. Sorry Big Al……

Next day we all went back to the pond, including Al, and the lady a the pay kiosk asked if we were going to throw that big daft boy in again? Of course we didn't, once was enough. I met Al a few years ago in Asda, and by god, you wouldn't dare try anything like that again….he has now gone from a lanky wee boy, to someone built like a brick shithouse!

We had a lovely lady called Nan Flannigan, who worked in the office at Kirklee Road. Nan was in the habit of parking her Mini anywhere she liked. One Friday, about a dozen or more of us physically lifted her Mini, and put it lengthwise between two trees with only a couple of inches to spare front and back. It wasn't there on the Monday, so I guess she got it out! Must have taken ages of too-ing and fro-ing to eventually dislodge from it's predicament!

Onto Gaulds of Glasgow now…..

We used to take any cars that were sold down South to the Motor rail terminal in Stirling. One time, I was just on the slip road to join the motorway, when I passed a hitch hiker. I pulled in about a hundred yards away from him. He must have though his luck was in, as I was driving a Rolls-Royce Silver Spirit. He picked up his backpack, and ran towards me. Just as he reached out for the door handle, I sped of, leaving him shaking his fist and no doubt shouting out some expletives!

Cruel I know, but I thought it was amusing at the time. Hope he's not still there!

Another time I was walking across the motor rail yard, and I noticed a broken wristwatch in a frozen puddle. I dug it out and kept it for some mischief later.

I need to go back to a joke I told a few weeks previously. It's the one about Paul Daniels at one of his shows. He asked for a volunteer from the audience, and this lad went up. Paul asked him for his wristwatch, which he put into a black velvet bag, and proceeded to smash it with a hammer. Much to the dismay of the volunteer, Paul emptied out the bag, only to be faced with a smashed up watch!

Paul profusely apologised to the chap, and arranged to meet him after the show. The chap and his wife met Paul afterwards, and Paul said that to make amends, he would take the couple to a very expensive restaurant, which he did. Paul ordered a mince pie, which duly appeared on a silver platter. Guess what was in the pie? Now at this point in my joke telling, Willie Curry blurted out "THE WATCH, THE WATCH" to which I replied "NO – MINCE!".….

We all had a laugh, but going back to the watch I found….At lunchtime one day, I had a mince pie and chips (pie supper). I hollowed out some of the pie, and put the watch inside, then covered it back up with the pastry. I ate the chips, and knowing fine well Willie would jump at the chance of a free meal, I said "I'm full up, does anyone want this pie?" Willie of course snatched it up and bit into it, only to nearly break his teeth on the watch. Oh how we all laughed, especially me as I was running for my life getting chased by Willie!

As we also had the Range Rover franchise, I was asked by big John to take a new Range Rover home, as the owner complained of bad starting, but only in the mornings. I lived in Beith, Ayrshire at the time, and took the car home. After tea, I said to Karen, my wife, who was eight months pregnant with our first child, "how do you fancy going a run in the Range Rover, and we can look at the new houses getting built at the other end of town?". Off we went, and as I was driving round the building site, all of a sudden the car sank in the mud. I had driven off a concrete plinth which had been hidden by the rain.

Shit! I couldn't shift the car, no matter how I tried. So, leaving Karen with the car, I ran back to the house, where I picked up my 450SEL Mercedes and a rope. I sped back to the site, and managed to secure a rope round the Range Rovers tow bar. Several yanks later, I managed to o pull the car out the mud and back onto hard standing. Back to the house with both cars. The Range Rover was up to the doors in mud, so I got up early and headed for work, after diagnosing a fault fuel pump for the bad starting. The car wouldn't go above 30mph due to a horrendous vibration coming up through the power train. Shit, I thought, something's got bent last night! Into work, thankfully nobody else there yet, I put the car in the wash bay and power washed it… low and behold, the vibration had been caused by a brick jammed in the alloy wheel.

That was duly kicked out, and the car was fine. New fuel pump duly fitted, the car was again put in the wash bay. Norman (Norrie) McKenzie (our cleaner and driver, not to be confused with Norman J McKenzie in the Murray Motor chapter), duly set about getting the car cleaned. Next thing I heard was him cursing…manky bastards he declared, as when the rear doors were opened, the door checks were full of mud. I never cracked a light!

Norrie was a good driver, but if there was something not right when he delivered a customers car, rather than taking it back to us, he would deliver the car, but tell the customer. He once said to a customer, the brakes aren't right, I wouldn't accept that!

Norrie did drive a Rolls-Royce for my wedding. I had been let down by a "friend" who was going to use his RR, so Gaulds very kindly gave me the use of a Shadow, registration BS66, which had been traded in by Bill Samuel, from whom I still receive a Christmas card. Gaulds also treated us to a night in a Loch Lomond hotel as a wedding gift. Sadly, Norman passed away many years ago…

Fuel pumps seemed to be an issue with the early Range Rovers, I once collected a customers car, but after a few miles, it cut out. I kicked the fuel pump and it burst into life, although short lived.
I was in the middle of nowhere, no mobile phones in those days, what to

do? I noticed a piece of fencing wire loose on a fence, so snaffled that and tied it around the fuel pump. The other end fed through the open rear window, and accessible from the drivers seat. Any time the car cut out, I'd give the wire a yank, the pump would whack off the chassis, and it would start up. Eventually got back to the garage.

One of my testing routes was to the old docks at Govan, which still had cobbled streets. This was not only handy for diagnosing rattles, but for practising my "J" turns, that is speeding up in reverse, slamming on the brakes while turning the steering, meanwhile changing from reverse to drive. Had to be done in the wet though. One time, I was showing off to an apprentice, and halfway through the turn, we hit a dry patch, the car came to a halt and went up on two wheels, almost toppling over. How would I explain that if it had rolled. Needless to say, I no longer did "J" turns!

Around the docks were some embankments which I tested the four wheel drive on. One day, Grant Purdie brought in his Jeep Cherokee Chief with a problem. I tested it up the same embankment, but I didn't realise the front and rear overhangs were so much more that the Range Rovers. I was well and truly jammed. Eventually with a great deal of too-ing and fro-ing, I managed to get the car free.
Grant Purdie, the owner will crop up again in another chapter.

Going onto the Murray Motor Company days, we had a driver come car cleaner called Simon. He was a nice guy, perhaps a bit naive, and had a Ford Capri which he always parked round the back. In the summer months (Scotland?) he would put one of those corrugated foil windscreen sun blinds on top of the dash to protect the interior from the blazing sun (Again, Scotland?). Now, Capris could generally be unlocked with a screwdriver, the locks were that poor. We used to unlock his car and put the sunscreen on the outside of the windscreen and lock the car up. We did this every day, and it was a hoot watching him at 5 o'clock, scratching his head and thinking he was going doo-lally! We ended up letting him in on the prank, don't know whether he was annoyed or relieved he wasn't going mad!

I once borrowed a new Bentley cool box from our sister company in Edinburgh, in the hope of a sale. When the customer saw it, he had a laugh, as it was the same as you could buy in Halfords at a tenth of the price, albeit minus a Bentley logo. I kept that cool box for months, before Alex in Edinburgh wanted it back. I sent Simon out to a local joke shop to buy a can of aerosol spiders web, and a dummy spider to put on the box before it went back. Simon duly returned with the aerosol spiders webbing, but instead of a dummy spider he brought a pack of toy banknotes! Why? He thought I'd said a dummy fiver. You couldn't make it up!

I once attended an Aston Martin training course, and had driven down with my then counterpart Gary Fantom in Bentley/Aston Martin Etc in Edinburgh. I always drove, due to my recurring car sickness. On the way back, Gary fell asleep (just as well I was driving!), and next thing I woke him up outside the Pepsi Max roller coaster in Blackpool! He point blank refused to go, but I grabbed him and didn't leave him any choice in the matter.

Photo of us on the Pepsi Max, cost claimed under training expenses!

Myself on the left, Gary Fantom on the right (Please note the matching Aston Martin jackets, and also the little dick behind, giving two fingers)

189

Moving forward to working at Bentley Glasgow, when we were at the old dealership in Townhead Street, every Thursday, after work, myself, Russell Forsyth, Stevie Murray, and wee Malky Lowe (RIP) would head down to the pub called "Sneaky Petes" at the Strathclyde golf range, for a pint or two and a few games of pool.

As Russell and I both took the M74 heading North to go home, we always took a short cut through the Hamilton motorway services. We would often race each other, and this particular evening, Russell was in his wife's Honda Accord, and I was in my 3 Series BMW. Russell was very competitive, and took the lead. I was very close behind him, and noticed him lose the rear end on the long sweeping right hander! He promptly lost control and managed to go nose first down the embankment, dislodging a drain as he went. Oops!

I drew up and got out to survey the damage. Turned out to be very light, but the car was stuck. While we were wondering what to do, a 38 tonne articulated lorry drew up, and the driver asked if he could assist. He promptly got a rope, and we tied it to the rear of the Honda, and onto the rear of his trailer. He managed to drag the car up the embankment, and back onto the road. As I said, very little damage, and after thanking the lorry driver, we headed home. Don't think we raced again after that!

My good friend Ian had bought a new Bentley Arnage, and he decided we would go on a pub crawl, with Stevie Murray, Russell Forsyth and myself, being dressed all in black was the only rule. The Arnage, driven by Ian's driver Dick, picked me up at my house in Kings Park. We then moved onto the pub in Mount Florida called Clockwork for a pint. Ian would then call Dick, and he would pick us up at the front door! Class!

After a few more stops, we reached the Fenwick Hotel (before the new bypass road was finished) and were greeted by the chap behind the bar, who turned out to be the owner. Over a pint, the chap asked why we were all dressed in black. "We're the Johnny Cash fan club on our annual night out", we replied. After another pint, we confessed we were really undertakers on our works night out and we had arrived in the company hearse. The chap overheard us talk about using the hearse socially, and the ensuing discussion about the tax benefit in kind if used for pleasure. Not if we kept the body in the back was the informed answer. It was decided to move on, said our goodbyes, and left in the Bentley, but with the hotel owner and staff staring at us out the windows. We thought it hilarious, wonder if they did.

A pub in Prestwick next, and the night was finished off in a nightclub in Ayr. Great night, and I still have the photographs!

One day, Stu the painter came to me cursing and swearing, as one of the next door BMW sales guys had really annoyed him. "What you up to?", I asked. "I've just ordered a penis enlarger and sent it to him at BMW!" I wondered why he had a mischievous look on his face! All mail etc to anywhere in the group is opened at head office, and then distributed to wherever it needs to go, so I primed one of my contacts at head office to be on the lookout for this "delivery".

It duly arrived and was ceremoniously handed over to the salesman. Boy, did he throw the teddy out the pram. He threw his company car keys at the sales manager and stormed out, saying something along the lines of "stick your job". I think he calmed down later, but I would have probably have played along with the joke if I was him.

One of my old friends, Eric Golumb, who I'd known since I was about 20, had bought a white Bentley Continental GTC which had a water leak in the boot, which was duly fixed. I sent Jim our driver down to Asda, to buy a leek from the vegetable counter. I put the leek in the passengers footwell ready for Eric to come and collect the car. When I handed him the keys, I mentioned there was still a "leak" in the passengers footwell. Gawd, talk about a drama queen! He was nearly greeting as I walked him to the car,. The greeting erupted into hysterical laughter as he saw the "leek" sitting on the carpet!

The "Leek"

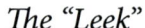

Another time, Eric had brought the car in for a rattle at the drivers door. It turned out to be no more than the junk he kept in the door pocket. I gave him an invoice, listing all the items we removed which were causing the rattle. This included a box of Tic-Tac mints, containing 27 mints, a set of keys, a pair of sunglasses, dental floss sticks, an aerosol deodorant, and many, many more things. You wouldn't get away with that with some customers, but Eric found it hilarious, and has kept that invoice to this day!

We were asked to assist with a Bentley to launch the opening of an upmarket jewellers shop in Glasgow city centre. I took a car along, and was joined by another Bentley and a Hummer, which was supplied by the security company who were running the show. I was standing blethering to Ian, one of the security guys, as there wasn't that much happening. There were a few onlookers, one of whom asked me what the occasion was. I replied that we were just waiting on Robbie Williams who was going to carry out the official opening ceremony (I just made that up, seemed like a good idea for a laugh!)

Within about ten minutes, the word had spread like wildfire, and the place was heaving, people hanging out office windows, all waiting to catch a glimpse of Robbie, who was never going to turn up!

At the garage in Townhead Street, we had taken in a Ferrari 360 Challenge Stradale, in Rosso with white racing stripes. One of the young sales guys had never been in a Ferrari, and as he was too young to drive due to our insurance restrictions, I took him out in it. The noise was incredible, we went up to the roundabout at Larkhall, then headed back. I opened the throttle and overtook 6 or 7 cars, at who knows what speed.

Shortly after returning to the garage, Ross Park pulled me up, saying someone had phoned in complaining about me. He asked how many cars I overtook. Thinking, if I'm getting my marching orders, I might as well go with a laugh, I replied "I've no idea Ross, I was going too fast!"

He laughed and that was that!

I've previously mentioned my pal Ian Weir (also best man at my wedding). One day Ian phoned me and said to come to his office right away. "Sorry mate, too busy here, how, what's up?" "It's okay, I'll be right down!"

He then appeared with all the girls from his office, all dressed in St Trinian's gear, you know, school uniform, stockings and suspenders…

He had told all his staff to dress for St Trinian's day, which the girls duly did. The guys were in on it, but dressed as normal. All the girls were good for a laugh, our male staff certainly enjoyed the spectacle!

This is perhaps not strictly high jinks, or indeed shenanigans, but well worthy of inclusion. I was due to attend another Bentley meeting, and my pal Neil Sawyers suggested we meet up with some of the Bentley technical guys, some of whom were retiring, and treat them to dinner and beer for all their assistance over the years.

A table was booked at a local pub down in Englandshire somewhere, but I was running a bit late, so phoned Neil and said just order me a hamburger. I arrived just in time to get this massive towering burger that Neil had jokingly ordered for me. Needless to say I got nowhere near finishing it... not even close.

Another incident where I wasn't sure of placement in this book was the time I opened up the dealership, and when I went round to the back workshop door, I noticed the Flying Lady missing from a Corniche in the yard. On further investigation I found some scuffs on bonnets, and a dent on the front wing of a new car. Looking up the CCTV, I saw a ned in a bright anorak climbing over the fence, and jumping from bonnet to bonnet over 5 or 6 cars, finally standing on the Corniche bonnet, and kicking pure fuck out of the mascot until it finally broke off. The cops were called in, but as the CCTV was not the best, we couldn't make out his face. He was last seen jumping on the boot of a Turbo R to climb the fence and escape.

Fortunately, he was wearing these big fancy trainers, with a spongy sole, which apart from minor scuffing did no damage to the cars. The scuffing was soon polished out, Willie Nicol, the dent guy fixed the dent on the wing of the new car, and I ordered a mascot from a second hand dealer down south, so all was good. I did inform the owners, but only after the cars were fixed. Next step was razor wire on the fence!

We once had a showroom event, where owners could buy Christmas gifts for their partners. The showroom was set out with various stalls, Harvey Nichols, exquisite form underwear, expensive perfumes and handbags, you get the idea…

There was a whisky distillers present, and they brought with them the "Angels Share" of a bottle that cost £5,000!! We had a "Wee Hauf" out of it, in the ideal glass where you cold savour the bouquet. That "Wee Hauf" cost in the region of £250… guy wasn't chuffed when I asked for some lemonade! We also had one of those chocolate fountain thingies, next to the fire exit. Someone opened the door and the wind blew chocolate all over a customers suit. "Just as well it was an old suit" I remarked. That went down well!!

Chapter Thirteen - Memorable Staff Members

I have had a great many memorable staff members, some memorable for the wrong reasons…
For those, I have changed their names to protect the guilty…

I have to mention one particular driver I had taken on it the Park's early days. Lets call him Jock. He was an ex traffic cop, six foot tall, very smart in appearance, but did lack a personality. One day, Jock was out the back of the Townhead Street garage, washing a customers car. Paul, one of our Skoda sales guys had brought a customer round to hand over his new car. The car had been prepared and ready to go, but being Autumn, fallen leaves had settled all over the car. Paul asked Jock if he could borrow the hose for a minute to wash the leaves off. Jock turned around and said "if you want the hose you can have it" and proceeded to turn the hose on Paul, soaking him to the skin.

Paul just stood there in disbelief, dripping! The customer did not know where to look, totally embarrassing.

I called Jock into my office and asked him for an explanation, only to be told it was only a wee drop of water. Sorry Jock, there's the door. I still don't know why he snapped, totally out of character.

Jock's replacement was found, a great chap called Harvey, ex accountant and very well organised. Harvey was with us for a good few years, one of these people you could trust do do something when asked. Harvey took my daughter Stephanie for her fourth time driving test, which she passed, and gave Harvey a big cuddle. Stephanie had been told by her driving instructor she would never pass, so I did a few weeks intensive coaching, and thought it better that Harvey took her for the test, less chance of nerves!

Harvey sadly retired, but passed on a folder he had made up, detailing all the customers addresses and directions to his replacement. I told you he was well organised!

I interviewed Harvey's replacement, lets call him George. Seemed to fit the bill, advanced driver, and a bit of a petrol head which was good. George was the son of one of our General Managers Porsche customers, very well to do, and high up in the medical profession.

I also needed a second driver, part time, so put an advert in the paper. You can imagine the response! Driving Bentleys and other supercars, and being paid! One particular applicant stood out more than the rest, and that was Jim Ross. He had taken the time to hand in his application in person, and I took to him right away. Jim was a retired chap, fitted the bill so was started. The part time position soon turned into pretty much full time, as we got busier and busier. At the time of writing, Jim is still with Bentley*, although on 3 days now, approaching his eightieth year. I play golf with Jim every Tuesday, and class him as one of my good friends.

*Jim has now fully retired as of June 2021, which means we now play golf during the day, instead of after work!

Going back to George, I once got a call from a customer, complaining that basically she had cracked a joke and George had not laughed! Gawd, some people. I told her I did not employ George for his sense of humour, but to drive and look after customers cars. That's her told!

Unfortunately, things were taking a turn for the worse with George, a few careless mistakes, damaging wheels, just minor things in the beginning which I managed to cover up, but as they became more frequent, he would have to cover the cost. He became a member of the "Fifteen Hundred" club, that is anyone causing a claim to be made had to pay the company excess of £1500 is it was deemed to be their fault. His membership to the club had been a result of running into the back of another car, in a Bentley he was bringing back from our bodyshop. Shame it was after the bodyshop repairs, and not before!

The final straw was when he collected a car from up North, and when he arrived at the dealership, drivers mirror was broken. At first he denied causing it, then changed his story to an articulated car transporter had cut a corner and hit the mirror. With his "description" of what had taken place, it would have been impossible to have happened as he said. I told him to wait in the canteen while we decided the next course of disciplinary action. He was seen to be making a telephone call to someone, presumably his father. He then stormed through my office, and in front of a customer threw his work mobile phone down, and walked out, muttering something about sticking the job somewhere!

Here we go again, but events were to take a fortunate turn. We often had drivers from other dealers dropping off cars, and one driver in particular,

Stuart Pottie asked me if we had any driver vacancies. Nice timing, a short interview ensued, and Stuart was hired. Another great move, Stuart is still with Bentley* and loving every minute. On his facebook page, he lists his profession as "Supercar Driver". Both Jim and Stuart are great assets to the company, and I am honoured to call them my friends.

At time of writing, Stuart is no longer with Bentley/McLaren, having been refused a pay rise, he is now driving part time for a pharmaceutical company, earning more than he did full time at Bentley. He will be sorely missed...

This book would not be the same without mentioning Ian McFadyen. Ian was a year or two older than me, and had a wealth of experience on the older cars. Ian would be the "go to" guy if any of the less experienced members of staff had a problem they couldn't resolve.

I have known Ian for many years, and he was also a talented photographer, indeed, he took all the photographs at my wedding. He was also the official press photographer for a local football club.

Unfortunately, mistakes do happen, and I remember Ian coming to me in June 2006, sheepishly admitting he had just smashed a customers Rolls-Royce. He had gone to move the Silver Spirit, to let an apprentice clean the workshop floor, and foolishly did not start the car up, but just put it into neutral, letting it run down the slope. Without the engine running, the car had little in the way of brakes, and ran down the slope, hitting the wall and fence. I watched the CCTV, and saw Ian, trying to stop a two and a half ton car with his feet! Accidents do happen, but he really should have known better!

I had to make the call to the customer, but it went very well, he said these things happen, and as long as the car was put right, he was okay. Ian had to join the 1500 club though!*

As mentioned elsewhere, the 1500 club refers to the company claiming back the £1500 insurance excess…

I also have to mention one of the best service advisors I have ever encountered, namely Michele Traynor, who I managed to "poach" from BMW when my previous advisor left to chase the "big bucks" at Mercedes.

Michele was not only great at her job, the customers loved and trusted her, and she also made my coffee….what more can you ask?

Chapter Fourteen – The Silver Ghost & The Bentley Blower

The Silver Ghost, AX201, Chassis number 60551 is arguably one of the most expensive cars in the world. There are other contenders for that title, perhaps the Ferrari 250GTO, or the Bugatti Type 57 Atlantic to name but two. AX201 was "inherited" by Volkswagen on their takeover of Rolls-Royce in 1998, and sold to a private individual in 2020 for an undisclosed sum. The good news is the car still resides in the UK. This is not a history lesson on this magnificent motor car, there are numerous publications on the subject, but more of my involvement with her during the course of my career.

The first time I met the motor car was when I worked for Gaulds of Glasgow in the early eighties. As a new dealer, we had "borrowed" the car for our opening. Disaster struck though, when we noticed a puncture in one of the front tyres. The factory was informed, and they rushed a new tyre to us. Now, this is not quite a job for Kwik Fit, instead it was entrusted to yours truly. Although not permitted to drive the car, I was allowed to get behind the wheel, and steered her into the workshop, pushed by our able team of staff.

Wheel off, and a *porta-power device was used to spread the wheel rim, allowing a spacer type wedge to be removed. This enabled the rim to be compressed, allowing the tyre to come off. Fitting the new tyre was the reversal of the procedure. Job done and back in action.

*A Porta Power is a hydraulic ram, with a hand operated pump, more used to car bodywork straightening.

The next time our paths crossed again was with Murray motors in North Street. Again as a new dealer, we borrowed AX201 for our launch. Again, not allowed to drive her, again I steered her into the workshop, using person power as opposed to horse power!

AX201 at Murray Motor Company in North Street

From Left to Right:
Simon Tennent driver/valeter, myself behind the wheel, and
Willie Curry Technician

The final time I was actively involved with the Ghost was at the launch of Park's Rolls-Royce and Bentley, in June 1999.

This was a very lavish affair, with a huge marquee erected in the grounds of *Cameron House at Loch Lomond. It was an impressive sight, with all the customers cars lined up, stretching along the grass leading up to the hotel.

Along with a full silver service dinner, there was entertainment laid on, and from memory, an early performance of the Red Hot Chilli Pipers. If it wasn't them, it was a group very similar. There was also a table magician, who managed to get his photograph taken beside AX201. Wish I'd done the same....

*Cameron House was sadly Ravaged by fire in December 2017, in which two people sadly lost their lives. The findings in January 2021 found that a night porter had caused the fire by placing hot fire embers in a cupboard which contained flammable material. Both the porter and Cameron House pled guilty to charges under the Fire of Scotland Act. The porter was spared a prison sentence, and given 300 hours community service. Cameron house was fined £500,000.

Spot the magician...

One of my hobbies is collecting model cars, initially based on Rolls-Royce and Bentley, and at this date, I have five models of AX201, and five other 40/50hp, which have also been called Silver Ghosts, based on the success of AX201.

My first wife had bought me a Franklyn Mint model of the Silver Ghost, many years ago, I reckon mid nineties. It unfortunately sustained severe damage during some furniture rearranging. I kept the pieces in a malt whisky tin for many years, until I retired, at which point I purchased another model for spares from eBay, and restored my original model, not quite on the scale of P & A Wood restoring Chassis 60551, but satisfactorily nevertheless. The model meant a lot to me, as my first wife sadly lost her fight with cancer several years ago

My very own Silver Ghost

The Bentley Blower has got to be one of my all time favourite motor cars. Like the Silver Ghost, this is not a history lesson, as there are many, many publications on the subject.

The original factory car has been totally stripped to the last nut and bolt, measurements taken, and from there, 1,846 individual parts have been hand crafted, enabling twelve customers cars to be produced. All twelve are pre-sold, cost is not mentioned, but is is certainly in the millions. 230 of those parts are actual assemblies, eg the engine, taking the total parts reproduced to several thousand. Car zero has been built, and at time of writing is undergoing extensive testing before the final customer cars are produced. This has caused mixed feelings among Bentley enthusiasts, as these cars, although mimicking the original, are mere copies with no history or provenance, and are merely a toy for the extremely wealthy. I certainly wouldn't turn one down!

I do however, have several Blowers in my collection in miniature, one of which I built from a rare Airfix 1:12 scale kit. I have 10 models of the blower, but this one is perhaps my pride and joy, probably because I built it…

I wasn't happy with the quality of the Bentley wings emblem on the radiator grille, so carefully bending to shape, I modified a Bentley wings lapel badge, and fitted that… much better.

My Airfix 1:12 scale Blower model.

The first time I was out in the Blower was at the factory in Crewe, it was raining and I'll never forget the feeling of being driven at what seemed like 80mph, with the rain stinging my face....what a buzz!

I've been out in it several times since then, both at the factory with customers, and at our Townhead Street dealership when I had got it on loan for a service clinic we were holding not long after we opened.

Latterly, I wanted to borrow it for a promotion we were having, but the costs by now were prohibitive, we would be billed for transportation both ways from Crewe, drivers time, hotel and expenses, and insurance. This amounted to several thousands of pounds, and not viable.
There was however, a solution, or so it seemed. One of our very good customers, Edward McGuigans grandmother was the oldest woman in Scotland at the time, at the ripe old age of 104, and a bit of a petrol head! A plan was hatched to get some publicity for Bentley Motors, and to get the Blower up to Scotland, if not free of charge, certainly at a reduced rate, and to have some form of press release with the lady and the Blower. Afraid to say, it never happened, I believe there was found to be another lady who was some 3 months older!

Chapter Fifteen – Car Sales

It is often said that the Sales department sell the first car, but the Aftersales department sell the next ones…..this is so true, a bad experience with the service department can jeopardise any future sales and customer loyalty. Some customers have a general distrust of car salesmen (or sales executives as they are now), sometimes this is justified, but more often than not, the sales guy wants to build a relationship with the customer, and will try to build up a trust.

I have sold a few cars in my time, two in particular spring to mind – The Bentley Brooklands two door coupe, a stunning motor car, both in looks and performance, and based upon the Bentley Arnage T running gear and powertrain. 0-60mph in 5 seconds, and a top speed of 184 mph from a motor car weighing in at some two and a half tonnes!

One of the most memorable of customers to show an interest in the Brooklands, was a Gentleman named Alexander Raeburn (Rae) Grieve. I first met Rae around 1999, when he bought a new Bentley Continental R from us. He had a criticism of the car however – there was no illumination of the gear selector, so at night, one had to go by feel, some may say a minor issue, but one I took seriously, as part of my job was to make sure the customer was happy with every aspect of his car.

I collected the car and brought it into the workshop. There was no way to get any integral illumination to the gearchange mechanism, so I had to come up with another plan. The recently introduced Bentley Arnage had a mini spotlamp in the roof consol to shine on the gearchange – I wonder if this car be adapted? One was duly ordered from the factory, and we stripped the roof consol, and managed to drill the veneer, and install the spotlamp, wired it up to the sidelamp circuit, and lo and behold, gearchange illumination! Looked as though it was a standard factory fitment, looks and worked great. Rae was delighted, and that was to stand us in good stead for years down the line. (No-one ever paid us for that work, but when someone spends over £150,000 on a car, it was the least we could do.)

Moving forward to 2007, the Bentley Brooklands was announced in the press. Rae phoned me, enquiring about the car, and I said one of our sales team would give him a call. I passed all the details to our sales (prevention) team. Two days later, Rae called me again, saying no-one had been in touch.

Disgusted, I said I would jump in a car and bring the information with me to his home farm in Lundin links, near to St Andrews. He said leave it until the next day, and he would take me to lunch. Next day, I jumped in my car (a Jaguar S Type), armed with all the information and a sales order form. I met Rae at his house and we went for a most enjoyable lunch at a local hotel.

Rae and myself at his local hotel for lunch.

I returned to the dealership with a signed order form and a deposit cheque for £25,000!

The next stage with this was a private viewing of the Brooklands down at Crewe, in the Mews, which was the private residence of the Bentley Chairman and CEO when he was over from Germany.

I took Rae and another likely prospect, in our demonstrator Arnage T, to a rather exclusive hotel, The Nunsmere Hall Hotel, where we had dinner, and a great night, a few drinks, a few cigars, and a lot of great banter.

I met that antiques guy off the telly, the orange tanned guy who's name escapes me (might have been Tim Wannacott). We were both standing out the front, having a cigarette (I smoked like a chimney in those days)

Earlier, we had noticed two rather attractive "ladies" driving up in a Ferrari, and they met up with this "gentleman" who was later recognised as a premier footballist. The were all the worse for drink at the end of the evening, and we saw the footballer carry one of the "ladies" up to his room, closely followed by the other "lady".….There may have been some money involved, but certainly no class!

Guess they were "ladies of the night" (and morning!)

The next morning after a very fine breakfast, we head to the Mews. When we arrived, we got the VVIP (Very VERY important persons) treatment, and had a good look around the Brooklands, followed by a very delicious lunch.

Rae behind the wheel of the new Brooklands at the Mews, near the Factory in Crewe – Tuesday 19th of June, 2007.

Another wander around the cars, at which point my good friend, Tim Hodgson (Customer VIP manager at Bentley) confessed to me that the customers were to be presented with a scale model of the Brooklands, as a souvenir of their visit. Only problem was the model cars had not arrived. When I went over to join Rae, he was deep in conversation with the Bentley Chairman and chief executive, Dr Eng. Franz-Joseph Paefgen, both of whom had great senses of humour as it turned out.
The conversation went something like this….

Rae: So Dr Paefgen, when can I expect my Brooklands? I also want it finished in pink!
Dr Paefgen: Mr Grieve, pink is no problem, and I can confidently say you will have a Brooklands by Christmas, but I cannot guarantee what size it will be!

At this point, Dr Paefgen had no idea that the model cars hadn't turned up, but I'm sure he guessed something was up, when Tim was standing behind Rae frantically mouthing "they've not arrived" and flailing his arms around like a propeller!

We all had a laugh about it later on the journey home. I let one of the others take a shot of the Arnage T on the way back, what a car that was.

Rae came into the dealership to spec his car, initially wanting the coachwork in green, but then changed it to a stunning Burgundy.

Anytime Rae telephoned in, he got Sally on the main switchboard, and Rae, being a right ladies man, was always flirting with Sally, all in good fun. The time came at the end of April, 2008 for Rae to collect his new Brooklands. Sally had bought him some furry dice for his rear view mirror, and came over personally to see him.

Rae was a cigar smoker, although never in his proper cars, that was kept for the Range Rover, but the first thing Rae did, was to put two large cigars in the centre consol, only there for emergencies!

More of these two cigars later.

Rae with Sally Anderson from our switchboard, April 2008

Rae later called me, when he got home with his new motorcar, everything was good, but he said he wasn't happy! Why, I enquired? "You took my photograph and never told me I had a hole in the elbow of my jacket!"

Rae and I became very good friends, and I was honoured to be invited over several years, to his "Birthday Lunches" at the local hotel, and latterly my wife Eleanor also attended, and she too was honoured to be one of his friends, although Rae always said I wasn't good enough for her, and why didn't she move in with him! He was just an old flirt.

Sadly, this was to be Raes final Birthday lunch………..

The Bentley Bentayga SUV was announced and Rae gave me a call. As there were no cars available to view, I called upon my good friend Tim Hodgson again. We arranged to have a pre-production Bentayga brought up in a covered transporter. I had another good friend and customer, Paul Veenhuijzen, who had also expressed an interest. We arranged for the transporter to meet us at Pauls home, Earlshall Castle, near Leuchars in Fife. Rae arrived to meet us, and we unloaded the Bentayga and they had a good look round it.

We then retired to the castles formal dining room, where Pauls good lady wife Josine had made a fantastic lobster bisque, which we all enjoyed with some fresh crusty bread. At the table was Rae, Paul, Josine, Tim, our transporter driver, also a young protege of Tims, and of course myself. After lunch, Rae asked our host Paul if he could smoke. Paul replied, "you are not smoking one of your cigars at my table!" I thought they were going to have fisticuffs, but then Paul said to Rae "You will have one of my cigars" and promptly disappeared to his smoking room to fetch two cigars from his humidor. The two of them lit up, and we were engulfed in a fog of cigar smoke. The young protege of Tims didn't know where to look, certainly a new learning experience for him!

Rae ordered a Bentayga, and was to send in a deposit of £5,000, and we would put him on the waiting list. The cheque (or so we thought) had not arrived after a fortnight, so I called Rae and he assured me it had been posted the following day. He called me back shortly thereafter saying the cheque had been cashed by our head office.

I went onto them, not happy, and eventually it came to light the £5,000 was sitting in the deposits account under A R Grieve, not one person had thought to ask if A R Grieve and Rae Grieve were one and the same person. Highly embarrassing.

Paul Veenhuijzen had, as well as his Continental GT, a very attractive classic 1961 Bentley S2 Continental which he was selling through a broker, and promised to have a Bentayga once the S2 was sold. The car at this point is still for sale at £395,000.

Rae very sadly did not enjoy good health, and passed away on the 5th of April 2016, never seeing his Bentayga, which was just about to start production. The production was cancelled, and the deposit returned to the lawyer handling his estate (who knew nothing about it!)

Myself, Eleanor, Sally Anderson from the switchboard and Tim Hodgson from the factory attended Raes funeral. He had a good 83 years of life.

Rae had no family to speak of, he left his collection of cars to his closest old friends, the Range Rover and the Carlhurlie estate went to his friend Catherine, who looked after him in all his years of poor health, and without her, Rae would certainly not have made 83. I'm not sure where his Ferrari ended up.

He had three Bentleys, all very special, and between them had around 4 or 5 thousand miles on the speedometers.

He had a 2002 Continental R Le Mans, one of only 12 right hand drive cars. Rae left that to his lawyer, who sadly passed away a couple of weeks later. The car was to be sold on…

He also had the Brooklands, which I had sold him, that was to be sold on……

Thirdly, he had the last retail production 2002 Bentley Azure T Drophead, which no sooner was Rae buried, the car was sold down south.

Now, I wasn't happy with the cars getting split up, they were Raes pride and joy, he hardly ever used them, but loved to look at them, rather like an art collector and one of his paintings!

I have another very good friend and customer, Davie Edwards, who is an avid enthusiast of the Bentley marque, so I arranged for him to see the two remaining Bentleys, which he duly purchased with my assistance. They had found a good home, this chap has some 8 Bentley motor cars, never used, just cosseted.

A few years later, Raes old Azure came into the hands of a dealer down south, Marlow Cars, and my friend bought it! All three of Raes Bentleys were now back together.*

The two cigars in the Brooklands? I have them proudly displayed in my cabinet along with some more of my treasured Bentley memorabilia.

*Since the time of writing, most of the cars have been sold, as the weren't getting used, and the owner who had just turned 70, found the cost of keeping them all taxed and insured very prohibitive...shame, but understandable

RIP Alexander Raeburn Grieve 3rd May 1932 to 5th April 2016

Now, Bentley motors could be that far up their own backsides at times. When the Brooklands was announced, there was a strict £25,000 deposit, and the car would cost full retail in the region of £250,000. The car although stunning, did not quite do as well as the planned 550 they were to produce. I had one customer who wanted one, but when asked for the £25k, he refused, saying he has bought many new Bentleys, as had his father and brothers, and if his word as a gentleman wasn't good enough, they could stuff it!

Several months later, I was speaking to the area sales manager for Bentley, and struggling to meet the numbers, he asked me, surely you must know someone for one of these cars?

I did, but explained the deposit situation, and he basically gave me carte blanche. I called my customer, and said why don't we meet half way as a goodwill gesture on both our parts? Within half an hour, he had sent a driver over with a cheque for £12,500!

Brooklands number two to me! That was the only two Brooklands sold in the West of Scotland, I got £250.00 commission, the company made £25,000 each car! Hmmmmm…..

Bentley didn't quite reach the 550, making only 426, or 432 if you include prototypes. Still a stunning motor car, and very collectable.

When the Mulsanne first was introduced, we got a stock car through for the showroom. The car was stunning, black coachwork with black interior. One of my customers who is sadly no longer with us, had an Arnage with the same colour scheme. I called him up and after the usual pleasantries, I announced his new car was here. After a momentary silence, he expressed surprise but agreed to humour me and come out and see it. He bought it! When he was leaving, he shouted to me across the car park "you made me by that you bugger" or words to that effect. Did me no harm, as it was within earshot of one of the directors!

This same customer, previously traded in his Silver Arnage for a black Arnage, on the understanding we would let him use a Silver car for his daughters forthcoming wedding, as black would not be quite suitable! We agreed, and when the time came, I drove the car to pick up the groom and best man, taking them to the owners house, where a magnificent wedding venue had been set up in marquees, including cloakroom, main banqueting and ballroom, kitchen, and balcony overlooking the impressive gardens of the house.

Job done, I had some time to kill, so started to ferry some of the guests from their homes to the venue….I knew most of them as they were also customers. The plan was to come back at midnight and take the newlyweds to their hotel. I arrived just before midnight, and was invited out to the balcony and witnessed a firework display that would put many an olympic display to shame.

Shortly after, I collected the newly married couple, and took them across the city to One Devonshire Gardens, where they would spend the wedding night before jetting off on their honeymoon. I only made one stop, to an all night convenience store, to buy them cigarettes, as they both smoked and had been "gasping for a fag" since before the ceremony. I was happy to pay for the ciggies, as the couple hadn't brought any money, and I had been generously rewarded by both my customer, and the guests I had collected.

All in all, a great and rewarding day. I have not mentioned the name of the family or the owner, out of respect for my late customer, who I have had the pleasure of knowing for some 30 odd years.

This next one is a bit spooky. I was in the showroom, and took a couple of images of a black Mulsanne to send to another customer. It was some time later that I noticed a third image, which I do not recollect taking. It looks like an image of my late mother, taken through the showroom window. She would appear to be floating above the ground, and wearing her pink dressing gown, her face being hidden, but the hair is the same….see what you think?

You can see the reflection of myself and flash reflected in the showroom window, but how can the image of my mum be explained?

You can see on the extreme left the rear of the Mulsanne I was photographing….

Spooky...

To add to it, the date the photo was taken was a year to the day from my mums funeral.......

Navtrak was the only authorised tracking device that could be fitted to Continental GT and derivatives. The sales prevention team were always incentivised to sell these units on every new car, sometimes these incentives were quite lucrative. One December, the sales manager asked if I could assist. They were three or four units short of target, and if I could sort that I would be included in the incentive. There was nothing underhand, it just meant the units I would normally fit in January would be squeezed into the workshop end of December, therefore meeting the target.

For that, I received £800 worth of Hugo Boss vouchers, as did the sales manager and two salesmen.

These came in handy, as I would not normally even consider such overpriced, albeit good quality clothing. Not bad, three pairs of jeans, a pullover, and the rest of the vouchers used up on underwear.

I'm including this in the sales section, as Paul Lilley was the Bentley Regional Sales manager from January 2009 until May 2012. Paul emailed me one day, asking if I was born in the South side of Glasgow.

"Yes" I replied, "Why?"

"Was it in Allison Street?" to which I replied "yes, why, are you stalking me?"

"Do you remember one of your neighbours, Wendy?" he asked.

"Yes of course, Wendy Godfrey, she was my first girlfriend" I answered.

"Be careful what you say about my **mother**" he responded!

Gawd, I was three or four years old, and Wendy would be about five. Next thing I knew, Wendy pinged me an email to say hello. I sent her a photograph of her with her arm around me, I was in my cowboy outfit (no remarks about still being a cowboy!) and Wendy was in her school uniform. Talk about a small world! Wendy and I still keep in touch, promising to meet up one of these days as she shares her time between Englandshire and France. One day though…..

I had bought a Land Rover Defender, just about the time Paul moved to Jaguar Land Rover, and I also own a Triumph Tiger motorcycle, and spookily, Paul changed his career to become General Manager of Triumph in the UK and Ireland. He's now manager with Harley Davidson, and I did own a Harley several years ago.

He's definitely stalking me! I've recently bought a classic Suzuki motorcycle, lets see if he now joins Suzuki!

Wendy and myself around 1958/9 in Allison Street, Govanhill, in the South side of Glasgow'

Wendy with the white ribbon in her hair, with myself on the extreme right hand side… Growing up as kids in the late 50's

In December 2011, we had arranged to borrow the Bentley GTC Supersports Ice Speed Record car (ISR) as a point of interest in the showroom. On the 28th of February 2011, driven by world rally champion Juha Kankkunen, the car achieved a speed of 205.48 miles per hour on the frozen sea off the west coast of Finland.

The car was delivered by transported to our dealership, and as soon as the truck was away, I jumped into the drivers seat (car was left hand drive) Lee jumped into the passenger seat, and we went for a drive around Hamilton…gawd if we had been caught either by the police or head office, we would have got our arses booted. Was fun though!

Yours truly and the Ice Speed Record car

Chapter Sixteen – New Model Launches.

Rolls-Royce Silver Shadow 11   21st February 1977

Not much to say on this, I was a lowly mechanic, and as such was not invited to the launch. I did however, get a commemorative ashtray with the words Appleyard and 21st February 1977.
Changed days now, as all staff are welcomed and encouraged to attend these things, good for boosting morale, and making everyone part of the team.

Rolls-Royce Silver Spirit 1996 model

I always remember this one....I had just returned to the official dealer network since finishing up RRS. It was in a castle in Wales I believe. It was evening, and we were all called outside to witness the cars driving in to the strains of Johann Pachelbels Canon in D major, and then accompanied by a fanfare of trumpets, the cars were spotlighted. I remember thinking "that paintwork is awful!"
The cars had been suffering from what we called the "hologram effect", causing swirl marks to produce a rainbow effect which looked terrible. Usually a good final glaze took care of it, but sometimes I felt the anger of a customer, in one particular instance, we had delivered a car back to the owners office after servicing, and he immediately rang me, going ballistic! "what have you done to my paintwork! The car is covered in scratches, it's ruined!
I reassured him, and immediately collected the car. An hour spent polishing and glazing the car and all was well. Car delivered back and I explained to the customer when we power washed the car, the hot water had removed any traces of polish, causing this effect, It looked far worse than it was, but alarming nevertheless. Customer was satisfied, and the cleaners warned not to blast the living daylights out the cars when service washing!

I would have thought Rolls-Royce Motors would have sorted this before they displayed the cars to us......

Rolls-Royce Silver Seraph Launch –

I cannot recall if it was Millbrook or MIRA, but we were driven there by coach from our hotel around midnight, as the Seraph was at that time still top secret. There were also European dealer delegates present, not just the UK. We were given turns driving the cars around the test circuit, then the word came back that the French delegate had crashed the car. It was returned to the facility, and the damage wasn't too bad, so the bumper was secured and the car returned to use.

Shortly after, word came in that the French had smashed the car again! This time the damage was more severe, and the car was out of action. The factory guys were raging, once was unfortunate, twice was bloody careless. This threw out the driving schedule, so the rest of us did not get as long in the car as we would have liked. You get idiots at almost all of these events, out to prove what a better driver they are than the rest of us. That's not the purpose, the purpose is to get the feel of the car and it's capabilities, which can be conveyed back to prospective clients.

The Seraph was so different from previous models, with it's V12 naturally aspirated power unit, and new suspension design, it was the first really new model produced since 1965.

10th March 1998 Edinburgh Castle 10th March 1998 – Official launch of The Silver Seraph.

As I was with Murray Motor Company at this time, and being an Edinburgh company, it was appropriate to launch the new car at Edinburgh Castle. I hired a kilt outfit, and drove through in the early evening. The weather was not kind, but we had a great time with the castle hospitality, then came the announcement for all guests to make their way outside to witness the new car. Umbrellas and sheltering were the order of the day, but what a magnificent sight – the new Rolls-Royce Silver Seraph being led by the pipe band, igniting pyrotechnics as it drove gracefully down the causeway.

Everyone received a traditional commemorative engraved quaich, courtesy of George Paterson, sales manager, who was largely responsible for the evening. I still have that quaich on display in my collection.

1999 – Bentley Hunaudieres

Although more a concept car than a new model, the car was built for the 1999 Geneva show. It was the motorcar that was the forerunner of the Bugatti Veyron.

When I first heard the name, I thought it was a wind up ie **Hun** as in a wartime nickname for a German, and **Audi** named after one of the group marques.

In reality, it was named after a famous straight on the "Circuit de la Sarthe (AKA Le-Mans 24 hour race track), where Tim Birkin in a blower Bentley overtook a Mercedes at 125mph, with one wheel on the grass!

The Hunaudieres, the forerunner of the Bugatti Veyron.

I had the pleasure of seeing this actual car in the flesh, at one of my many factory visits. It did have a puncture in the nearside front tyre, but the tyre and wheel were of a one-off unique design that couldn't be repaired. They were waiting on a new wheel and tyre!

The New Continental GT launch, 2003 at India of Inchinnan.

The saviour of Bentley was about to be launched, the new Continental GT. Bentley dealers had all been losing money hand over fist, and this new car was to be the answer, and it certainly was, the first cars getting well over list price, certain dealers making up "ghost" customers to secure more cars. Not that we ever did that!

The launch venue was to be in Scotland, India of Inchinnan to be precise, a stunning, totally restored Art Deco building designed in 1930, that once was the home of India tyres.

This was to be our home for the UK dealer conference in the afternoon prior to the launch evening.

All the dealer delegates met in Glasgow the previous evening, to be hosted by Bentley and treated to dinner, followed by a night in a top hotel. All went well, until we tried to check into the hotel. Myself and *Malcolm Lowe from sales had our bookings cancelled, someone at Bentley had assumed that because we were local, we would be going home – Aye right! Soon put them straight on that one.

A great night was had by all, good food, good company, and as usual, copious amounts of alcohol.

The launch event was not only for dealers, but for customers and prospects who had never seen the car in the flesh. My great friends, Ian and Tracy picked us up in their new Bentley Arnage, and chauffeured us to the venue. Tracy was driving, as she was some 8 months pregnant, thus the designated driver for the evening. It was a stunning location, and Bentley did these things well in those days. Alcohol was flowing, specialist cocktail makers were in abundance to make up anything you desired. I must admit to partaking of several.

The new GT was amazing, and very well received by all. Unfortunately, all good things must come to an end, and trust Tracy, she found her way to the back door, skilfully manoeuvring the Arnage around various fountains and ornamental ponds. We were suitably collected and driven home safely. Thanks guys.

Malcolm Lowe (Wee Malky) very sadly passed away in December 2020 from a combination of Covid and Pneumonia.

One of my earliest memories of Malky was of him and Stevie Murray play wrestling outside Sneaky Petes pub, which was down at the Strathclyde Park Golf range. I don't know who flung who, but one of them ended up on Malkys company car bonnet, denting it! Oops! Fortunately, Willie Nicol, one of the original dent repair specialists came to the rescue, and sorted it out before head office got wind of it.

Malky was a great wee guy and my sincere condolences go to his widow Karen and all his family.

RIP Wee Malky

2005 First Generation Continental Flying Spur.

Off to Millbrook for the testing of the (at the time) Continental Flying Spur. We took turns in driving the car on the Alpine circuit, which gave a very broad spectrum of driving conditions, as the name suggests. I was sitting in the back, a Bentley driver in the front passenger seat, and Pedro Silva, one of our sales guys was driving. Pedro started going faster, despite the instructions from the Bentley guy to slow down. We were getting flung about in the back, and at times I thought either the car would overturn or I would throw up. Hopefully not at the same time. The Bentley driver (and me) had had enough, Pedro was ordered to slow down, which he ignored, shouting and giggling that he was having fun. The Bentley guy pulled on the parking brake, which has the effect of doing a controlled emergency ABS stop, which soon put paid to Pedro's antics!

March 2005 Continental Flying Spur showroom launch.

We had a showroom launch for the Continental Flying Spur in March 2005, which was very well attended, we had only just moved into the new premises, and as mentioned in another chapter, the showroom floor hadn't even been tiled!

Cyprus Green – who picks that colour for a launch car?

June 2006 Continental GTC – Showroom Launch Event

We had a very successful launch for the new Continental GTC, and employed the services of a magician to mingle and do some close up magic. His name was L'etoile, who later was to get booed off the stage in Britains Got Talent. He was excellent, but I fear that his type of close up magic did not transfer well to the stage! Anyway, once all the guests had gone, all the staff and L'Etoile stood around a desk, and chewed the fat.

Being an amateur magician, I was keen to show off my talent to a professional. I do a routine where a volunteer cuts a length of rope, and I "miraculously" join it together. Now, not having any rope or scissors, I scavenged a length of electrical cable, and a pair of pliers was used to cut it. Without giving away any secrets, the trick ended with a bit of slight of hand, secreting a piece of wire into my jacket pocket. I forgot that I was wearing a new suit, and the pockets were still sewn up. I hastily threw the piece of wire behind me, which went unnoticed to all, except big Al the general manager, who erupted in laughter.

The real magician then borrowed big Al's suit jacket, and asked if anyone smoked. I did at the time, and gave him a cigarette, which L'Etoile lit up and started smoking. He cupped Al's jacket in his hand and flicked the cigarette ash into it. Finally, he stubbed out the cigarette into the jacket, much to the horror of big Al! L'Etoile then handed the jacket back, and lo and behold, not a mark on it. The magician beat a hasty retreat, no doubt to run some cold water over his hand, which I reckon he stubbed out the ciggy in!

Left to Right:
Big Al Paterson
Myself
Neil McCallum
John Green

January 2010 – Mulsanne showroom Launch

The band of the Royal marines, and at the rear from left to right: Myself, Neil McCallum, Colin Wright, Lee Martis and Russell Graham

Paul Lilley from Bentley nearest the camera, along with Neil McCallum unveiling the new Bentley Mulsanne.

2010 Continental GT Supersports.

We were invited to Millbrook testing ground for what was to be one of the most impressive insights into a new model, the Continental Supersports. This at the time was the fastest ever Bentley, the ultimate Bentley, something we would get a sample of in the hours to come.

As usual, our mobile phones were taken off us, as there was usually some manufactures secret new model being tested. We were then split into groups, each allocated a specific part of the days agenda, and given a lanyard with out team details. There were several hours in the classroom, learning about the new car, then the fun part. We headed down first of all to the mile straight, where there was a selection of exotica waiting for us. Amongst those most memorable were a Ferrari 599, a Porsche 911 Turbo, and of course the new Bentley. There was about 5 or 6 cars there, but these are the most memorable.

We each had a turn at flooring each car, to see how fast we could go on the mile straight before we had to brake. We did of course have one of the Bentley drivers with us to keep us right!

I remember, using launch control, the Porsche reached just over 170mph, the Ferrari reached 177mph, and the Bentley managed a paltry 166mph….Not bad for a car weighing almost two and a half tonnes. I have to say though, the Bentley with its weight and all wheel drive, was the most stable and sure-footed of all the cars I tested. It did have however, 621 brake horsepower, giving it a 0-60mph time of just 3.7 seconds. This was also the first Continental GT to have the all wheel drive configuration changed to 40% front and 60% rear, from 50/50, making it much more of a drivers car.

This was the time I had the privilege of meeting Derek Bell, 5 times Le-Mans winner and a myriad of other titles to his credit. I could tell by looking at him what a life he must have led. He would have been around 69 or 70 years old at this time, and he just had the look of someone who had lived life to the full in the world of high end motorsport, his face was wrinkled and had the look of tanned leather, no doubt due to many years of sunshine, and the jet set lifestyle. His hands, as I remember were massive, and on his wrist was a Breitling watch, with a face the size of Big Ben!

What a lovely guy he was, and while chatting, I mentioned how great it would be to be a passenger in a car he was driving. No sooner said than done…..We went around the test circuit in a Supersports, with Derek at the wheel. We all think we are good drivers, some more than others, but when you are in a car with a racing driver, you realise how average you really are. I still have a promotional DVD of Derek driving a Supersports around the Nurburgring.

Next, I took a Supersports around the banked high speed bowl, which was in a circle of 5 lanes, covering a distance of 2 miles. You could be in the outside, most banked lane, and the car could be steered by using a combination of speed and centrifugal force. You had to be going pretty damn fast though, reckon I was doing around 160mph, and it would take way less than a minute for the two mile marker to come around.

We also drove the car around the Alpine circuit, which is just over 4 miles of simulated hilly mountain roads, and then it was back to the classroom. One of the instructors then appeared with four crash helmets, and the top four dealer delegates who participated in an earlier quiz, were led away. What's going on we all wondered, as we boarded our coach for the return journey to our hotel. All of a sudden, the coach stopped at the barrier beside the high speed bowl, at which point, we were asked to disembark.

We lined up a few feet from the barrier, then we heard in the distance this incredible sound. It was four Supersports, side by side, driven by the *Bentley drivers, with the lucky delegates in the passenger seat. Before we knew it, they were coming around again, but this time nose to tail at 185mph! The noise was awesome, I'll never forget it as long as I live….no wonder Bentley is in my blood.

* *The Bentley drivers were a great bunch of blokes, most of whom were racing drivers.*

2010 GTC Supersports Launch.

2010 saw the launch of, to this day one of my favourite models, the Continental GT Supersports Convertible.

We were invited to the dealer launch, which was to drive from the Crewe factory, to Portmeirion in Wales, and to get us there was a fleet of around 6 or so, Supersports convertibles, all in the colour "Citric", which was a sort of light green....sounds terrible, but they looked stunning. We were to take turns at driving, but I am the worlds worst passenger, getting car sick if I'm not driving. This soon became apparent as we had to stop a few times on the way there, to allow me to throw up! After a fantastic afternoon and lunch at Portmeirion, it was time to head back. As word of my "ailment" soon spread, it was decided to let me drive all the way back....I wonder why?

Picture this, a beautiful day, sun splitting the sky, driving one of the worlds finest cars on country roads with the hood down....does life get any better?

January 2011 New Model Continental GT – Club Marbella.

For some reason I was delayed in getting to the Club Marbella, and everyone had eaten. I was forced into drinking whisky on an empty stomach, which had an adverse effect on my ability to walk straight. Well I managed to walk straight - straight into a palm tree!

I told everyone it was a reset button on my forehead…….. Fortunately my various hats covered the battle scar!

The following day was test driving the new GT, as usual, me being a terrible passenger, caused me to throw up. I should write a tourist guide on where the best places to vomit are.

Me shielding from the sun.....
(Not hiding my embarrassment in any way!)

That evening was a bit special. We were each given an apron and a chefs hat, and split into teams. Each team was given a rather large Paella pan and various ingredients. We were to make a Paella, depending on what ingredients we had. Some were meat, some chicken, seafood, vegetarian etc etc. Our team won! I still have the hat and the apron. More about aprons in another chapter.

Another eventful trip over, heading back home the next morning.... another day, another hangover!

January 2011 New Second Generation GT Showroom Launch.

There was a lot going on that afternoon, the showroom was cleared to allow a specialist lighting company to erect an elaborate framework around the new car, along with the lighting to create some spectacular effects, one of which was the illusion that the car was racing along the road, wheels looking like they were rotating. I have this on video, but unfortunately you guys cannot experience it in this book!

The framework all fixed up, ready for the evening launch

Great turnout , the best is yet to come...

The next couple of photographs give you an idea of some of the effects, bearing in mind it is the same motorcar.

11th April 2013 Next generation Flying Spur – Anglesey Race Circuit

As usual with Bentley, we were put up in a top hotel, and we were taken to Anglesey circuit, driving the second generation Flying Spur. The circuit was wet, but that just went to show how capable the car was. In the evening we were taken on a VIP tour of Liverpool Football ground, where I had my picture taken with some trophy or other….you may guess that football and me aren't quite the bedfellows that some of my colleagues are.

15th January 2015 McLaren Glasgow Launch.

This is referred to in another chapter….

November 2015 Bentayga SUV – Marbella

It was announced that I would be attending the worldwide launch of the new SUV (Sports Utility Vehicle), which was to be named "Bentayga". Personally I thought they should have resurrected one of the classic Bentley names, or perhaps named it after one of the famous "Bentley Boys", as they did with the "Birkin" version of the Arnage. Anyway, not my decision. Apparently the name drew inspiration from the first three letters of Bentley, and the altered spelling of "Taiga", which is the worlds largest transcontinental snow forest. Curiously, the word "Bentayga" also means "carried interest" in Swahili! The other theory is that it was named after the Roque Bentayga, which is a big chunk of rock in Gran Canaria. There you go, every day is a school day.

I was going with Derek, one of our sales team, Derek is one of the good guys, and we still keep in touch. Derek (Del) met me at my house as we were flying from Edinburgh airport, and it made sense as I was a third of the way there. We met one of the guys from Bentley Edinburgh, and after breakfast we boarded the plane bound for Malaga.

Soon, we were met at the airport by a chauffeur driven Bentley, and whisked to Marbella, Club Marbella to be more precise. Bentley apparently had taken over the full hotel, paying for any guests already there or booked in, to be put up in one of the other nearby luxury hotels. There was, however, one snooty couple who point blank refused to go, maybe they regretted not moving once the whole restaurant and bar were taken over by the rabble that was worldwide Bentley dealers! I remember the couple looking a bit out of place, sitting at a wee table in the corner of the restaurant.

Del and myself had a few drinks that evening, but not that many (Hmmmm), as we were driving the following day, also, club Marbella certainly knew how to charge, from memory it was something like 25 Euros for a Brandy! (More of that later) Not really claimable on company expenses….

Next day, after breakfast, we were split into groups of four, and after a briefing, we were installed in a Bentayga, with Ascari Racetrack programmed into the satellite navigation.

The briefing basically said that it any warning lights came on, stop the car, restart, and if the light went out, good to go. If the light did not go out, we were to phone the Bentley team, and they would send help. I will mention that they were pre-production vehicles, not quite the final product.

I was first behind the wheel, been a while since I had driven on the "wrong" side of the road, but took off no problem, that is until a minute later, the suspension warning light came on! I did as Bentley advised, and restarted – all was now okay.

We would be taking it in turns to drive, not something I was looking forward to, given my motion sickness, but I had taken a "pill" so hopefully all would be fine.

It seems to be the norm with sales guys to drive like a nutter, watch me, see how good a driver I am, bloody idiots!

Anyway, we arrived at Ascari, but the off road track, not the race circuit – bugger! I was later to sample that with McLaren. It was good though, the car went through its paces well, as good as any other 4 wheel drive out there in the marketplace. The course was pretty safe though, allowing for the aforesaid mentioned bloody idiots. Guess they didn't want any mishaps. Must admit it was pretty tame compared to my escapades in my Land Rover Defender.

We returned to Club Marbella, without any further hiccups, and promptly installed ourselves in the bar. After a couple of drinks, time to go and get freshened up for dinner. One barbecued almost raw fillet steak later, we headed once more to the bar. Our colleague Neil was to meet up with us in the evening, the theory was to stagger the delegates, thus leaving our dealerships with at least some sales prevention representation.

The thought of buying rounds of drinks at extortionate prices didn't much appeal to us thrifty Scots, so Del had the brainwave of us buying a round or two, then "bunging" the waitress a rather large tip to look after us. This she certainly did, but only when her manager wasn't looking!

I had had enough, and left Del and Neil to carry on, keeping alive the good old Scottish tradition of drinking more than anyone else.

Next morning, alarm went off, I phoned Del to be greeted with "aye, ok, am up!" I arrived at the reception having foregone breakfast, no sign of Del. Our Bentley was at the door waiting to take us to the airport, still no sign of Del, even after many phone calls. I collared a porter, and we jumped into a golf buggy and headed for Dels room. Anyone who has been to Club Marbella will know it covers a fairly large expanse of land, and Del was down near the bottom. The porter opened the door with his pass key, and we found Del still in bed, out for the count. No time to wasted, I dragged Del up, (averting my eyes) as he must have forgotten to bring his pyjamas, and flung some clothes at him, while I shovelled the rest of his stuff into his suitcase, making sure we had his passport etc.

We just made our flight by the skin of our teeth, our fellow traveller from Bentley Edinburgh must have been somewhat concerned to say the least (politeness prevails here).

We were flying via London, so we all had a big breakfast at Heathrow, and that perked us all up. We had a bit of time to waste, so did the rounds of the shops in terminal 5. Del had promised his good lady a bottle of Cristal Champagne, but surprisingly there was none to be had. I spent some of my Hugo Boss vouchers from a previous reward, and we headed back to Edinburgh.

I drove back to my house, where Del collected his car and drove home. We reckoned it would be okay, as it was now mid afternoon, so hopefully the effects of alcohol would have worn off – Aye, right!

2018 – Third Generation GT launch

This car made a major change in it's construction, using superformed aluminium, don't think we did much launch-wise, but I did get to use one for the weekend when I retired…

I definitely think this car was a backward step, I still preferred the previous V8, in particular the GT3r.

Anyway, fat chance of me owning one now…

I must mention briefly Overfinch, an "upmarket" upgrade to Range and Land Rovers. We had the franchise which proved quite lucrative in the beginning, but tailed off, largely due to the poor product and warranty. How do you explain to a customer that all four alloy wheels are corroded due to the tyre pressures being too low? This according to Overfinch when we tried to get new wheels under warranty. They were talking shite!

A limited edition Overfinch Range Rover Holland and Holland at our showroom launch…

(The two models were not included)

We stored the Overfinch kits at our bodyshop, as we didn't have the room. One day, I got a call from one of my pals in the bodyshop, saying someone was stealing parts from the kits. In this instance, it was a rear spoiler valued about £900. My pal was telling me that none of the genuine guys in the shop wanted associated with the thief, or tarred with the same brush. The thief had advertised the spoiler on Gumtree for £300, so I informed head office. A sting was planned, a used range rover was borrowed to add credence to the plan. The advertised number was called, and the lads wife answered, arranging to meet, and gave out the address. Bingo! It matched the suspected member of staff, he was duly hauled in and fired. No further action was taken, no doubt Park's didn't want the bad publicity. At the time of my retirement, Overfinch was getting phased out, due to mainly cost and quality, and the previously mentioned warranty issues. Also, new Range Rovers were very expensive, and owners were reluctant to spend another £26k on Overfinch. Plus the fact, the new cars were very stylish as they came as standard, so didn't need anything further. Another headache away!

Chapter Seventeen - The Retirement....

I had planned to retire when I was 66 in August 2021, so around August 2018, I decided to give up my company BMW 5 Series, for two reasons. Firstly, it was costing me around £250 per month in tax, and secondly, if I retired in 3 years as planned, I would have to hand back the company car and get the bus home. I didn't even know where the bus stop was!

I always fancied a BMW Z4 since I had the use of one for a weekend a few years previously. Our sister company, Douglas Park BMW next door to us had the very car. I managed to get a good discount, and went ahead on a 3 year finance deal, which didn't cost that much more compared to the tax I was paying.

I had bought Melvin Johns Silver Shadow as mentioned previously in the chapter on memorable customers.

Melvin Johns old Shadow 11 MJI 5050

I kept the car for a year, and took it into Bentley for it's MOT. While there, having passed the MOT, a McLaren customer enquired whose car it was. I was introduced to him, and I sold him the car! I was planning on selling it anyway, as the coachwork was starting to show signs of corrosion, and although anything mechanical wasn't a problem, I hadn't planned on refinishing the car.

I also bought a Bentley T2 from an "ex" friend of mine. It needed a fair amount of mechanical work, but as I said, that wouldn't be a problem. The car was never destined to be mine. I had arranged for our transport department to collect the car and take it to our house in Nemphlar. The driver called me to say the car was delivered, but had rolled off the back of the lorry into a neighbours car! "Aye right!" I thought it was a wind up. In all seriousness, it had! We were doing you a favour the driver said, so claiming insurance wasn't going to happen. I had always wanted to pay for the transport with a discount of course, but I believe if the delivery went without a hitch they would have no hesitation in charging me. Maybe something to do with company policy of charging the driver a £1500 excess on any claim. There were quite a few members in the "£1500 club"

Turns out, the driver had just taken the securing straps off, and put the car into neutral, but as it had no brakes without the engine running, it ran away from him into my neighbours mothers car. He had been warned about this, but still paid no heed, didn't listen or maybe just didn't think.

To add insult to injury, it was a neighbour I had fallen out with some years before, and never spoke!

Before I bought the house in Nemphlar, the neighbouring farmer used to let his geese, ducks, chickens and even sometimes goats wander about loose, and invariably ended up in our garden, making some mess, digging up the lawn, and doing there business anywhere. When I bought the house, I pulled up our farmer neighbour, had a "word" and warned him in no uncertain terms to keep his livestock away. Never spoke after that, but he heeded my "warning". Anyway, I digress. If the Bentley hadn't hit her car, it would no doubt have careered down the hill, causing untold amounts of damage. So a blessing really!

You've heard me mention my friend Stu the Painter, who came to my rescue. I took the neighbours car in one Friday shortly afterwards, got to say it was one of the worst journeys ever! Being a farmers car, it was stinking, I guess the last passengers were sheep! Stu replaced the front wing, bumper and repaired the damage. I had the car cleaned from top to bottom, and took it back that evening. I won't say our neighbours became good friends, but we always spoke and gave a friendly wave after that. The Bentley only suffered a broken tail lamp and a scuff on the bumper. The fuel pump packed in shortly after, and had to be replaced.

My love for this car was becoming tarnished. It had just been repainted in the original colours of Cardinal Red over Garnet not long before I bought it, but as the months went by, I noticed the whole car was covered in micro-blisters, commonly caused by dampness in the primer when the car was repainted. I went back to my "friend" whom I'd bought the car from, and he didn't want to know. It was his own paint shop that had repainted the car. He is now an ex friend.

I sold the car shortly after that to a gentleman down South. Afraid to say I made a substantial loss, but I'm a perfectionist, and the car would never have been right without spending a princely sum to make it so. The gentleman who bought it was happy, and I had been totally honest about all the issues with the car. So much for retirement projects…..

The Bentley T2
Going to it's new owner
Can't say I was sorry to see it go…

Things got on top of me at work, too much pressure which I didn't need, and a lot of changes going on with Bentley. The Hybrid cars were just around the corner, and some of the criteria required were more than I wanted to be involved with. I brought my plans forward by about two years and handed in my notice towards the end of January. Relief!

On the 4th of February 2019, I finally left the motor trade, it was like a weight had been lifted off my
shoulders.

I recommended my friend and colleague from Honda to take over from me, which he did. I went back into the garage for a few days to ease the handover.

It was organised that there would be a meal in the Spice Restaurant along the road on the following Friday, to give me a send off….everyone was there, my pal Ian collected myself and Eleanor in his Bentley. All my friends and colleagues were there, got to say it was quite emotional, but I hid it well (I think).

Ironic that my first interview with Parks was in the very building where I had my send off…...

They all chipped in and bought my wife Eleanor and myself a weekend at Portavadie, on the shores of Loch Fyne, and gave me the new Bentley Demonstrator in which to travel. What a fantastic couple of days, finished off by a parcel arriving at the hotel. It was a scale model Bentley Continental R Fastback, which I had admired in the display cabinet.

I also met Carol Jagielko, who along with her husband Henry, were owners of the resort, but also good customers, having two Bentleys, and numerous McLarens. I got good wishes and a cuddle from Carol. Truly nice people.

I also received many gifts and good wishes from the guys which I treasure.

The plan was to get another job, with less responsibility. I had a couple of job offers, but I thought I'd give it a while before I jumped into anything.

I had sorted out my various pensions, and David my financial guy had amalgamated all my pensions into one pot. I had a pleasant surprise with one of them. I had taken out a pension when I had RRS, but I stopped contributions when the company was wound up. I had thought there was maybe about five or six thousand in the pension, but it turned out to be worth forty six thousand! I didn't need to work if I didn't want to!

I organised a barbecue at the house as a wee thanks for all my team and a few customers and friends. Even the rain didn't spoil it, we just moved into the garage and house. Was a great day, well before this Covid carry on.

At time of writing, I'm still living an idle life.
I keep busy, still get up early, this Covid has put a damper on things, but there are many worse off than myself.
In October 2020, I sold my house in Kings Park, Glasgow, which had a good bit of equity. I'd had that house since 17th of August 1998, it was sad to see it go, but I didn't need two houses, and the money came in handy. I paid off my car, and any other finance I had, and was left with no debt, great position to be in.
I spent a chunk of it upgrading our house in Nemphlar, and also funded one of my step daughters to take on the Broomgate cafe in Lanark of which I am now a director. I also gave some money to my two offspring, Roy and Stephanie just to give them a wee boost during these crazy times.

I still collect model cars, and have over 250 at present. I also make tables from car wheels, mostly Bentley and McLaren, I've sold a few to date, but just for some pocket money.
I still have my Triumph Tiger motorcycle, only done 14,000 miles since new in April 2007. I recently bought a 1978 Suzuki GS850, which is almost identical to my first big bike when I passed my bike test back in 1979. First time out, got done for speeding (40mph in a temporary 30mph limit). I appealed it as I reckon the speedo is inaccurate, but the procurator fiscal just doubled my fine and gave me 3 penalty points!

I still get a bit of golf in, although limited to good weather. During the summer, I meet with one of my old drivers and friend, Jim Ross every Tuesday, and we have a round at the Strathclyde park course. When I started writing this book, Jim was still driving for Bentley Glasgow at the age of 79, the customers loved him, a great guy and asset, he was talking about retiring though, I'll believe it when I see it.** Jim drove one of the wedding cars when I got married. I forgive him though……..

*Jim has now reached the ripe old age of 80, and has finally retired...

May 2019 RREC Scottish Section

Peter Gentles, After Sales Manager Extraordinaire

After 48 years working with Bentley and Rolls-Royce, Peter Gentles, After Sales Manager with Bentley Glasgow, has decided to retire. I first started dealing with Peter 27 years ago. My first impressions were of a warm, affable and confident man. As the years rolled by, I began to realise that Peter was also a brilliant engineer who could turn his hand to anything. Most recently even McLarens and Maseratis. Nothing phased him.

Those of you who have been lucky enough to know Peter will also know he has a wonderful sense of humour and is great fun to be with. I once had the privilege of accompanying him to the factory in Crewe. I laughed all the way there and back. It was a great couple of days. I also learned that Peter had owned a beautifully restored Rolls-Royce Silver Cloud. I have seen photographs of the car and it was stunning. When I asked him what happened to it, he replied that someone once offered him a great deal of money for it and with a young family he decided to sell. I think there are times when he wishes he had kept it.

Peter's shoes will be hard to fill. I doubt there are many people nowadays - or ever - with the technical and interpersonal skills Peter possesses. We all wish him well in his retirement.

The cartoon above, perhaps personifying the "Gentles" approach to his customers and their cars, was sent in by Gérard Le Clerc. And thanks to Irene Begley for the lovely image on the right.

HAPPY RETIREMENT
PETER GENTLES

18

My thanks go to Gerry and Irene Begley, for this touching tribute in the Rolls-Royce Enthusiast's club Scottish section magazine…..

Chapter Eighteen – And Finally

Summing Up.......

When I first began my career, there were 85 Rolls-Royce and Bentley dealerships in the UK, 71 in England, 7 in Scotland, 1 in Northern Ireland, 1 in Eire, 3 in Wales and 2 in the Channel Islands. This, of course was before the Rolls-Royce and Bentley parting of the ways in 2002.

Currently at time of writing, there are 25 Bentley (and Crewe built Rolls-Royce) dealers in the UK, 20 in England, 2 in Scotland, 1 in Northern Ireland, 1 in Wales, and 1 on the Isle of Man.

There are 8 Rolls-Royce dealers in the UK, only one of which is in Scotland. In total, this means that representation has declined from 85 in 1970, to 33 in 2020.......

The Rolls-Royce and Bentley franchises, and indeed I think, the whole of the franchise network is not what it was...there is no more enjoyment to be had.

Everything now is focussed on profit (Greed), led by accountants, and too much emphasis is placed on technicians efficiency. I was always customer focussed, and made some good friends amongst them, indeed, inviting some of them to my wedding. How many dealerships can say that?

Pretty much all the old school are now gone, especially from Bentley in Crewe and McLaren, where I have made a lot of good friends, and also in the dealer network.

We still keep in touch, and occasionally play golf or meet up for lunch at some mid-way point, just for a catch up and a good blether, putting the motor trade to rights!

Retiring after 48 years was a great move, I would have loved to have made the half century, but my time had come in the motor trade, I was a dinosaur, and there is no room for dinosaurs in the game now.....sad.

I have to say that I was disappointed that Douglas Park didn't take two minutes out of his busy schedule to pick up the phone on hearing of my retiral. Maybe I was just another number in the grand scheme of things?

In closing though, I have had some great times, travelled to many exotic and beautiful destinations, driven some fantastic motor cars, had some